Sexuality in Role-Playing Games

T0383608

"An exemplary look at an understudied facet of both role-play and digital sexualities."
— *J. Tuomas Harviainen, University of Tampere, Finland*

Role-playing games offer a chance to pretend, make-believe, and share fantasy. They often invoke heavy themes into their game play: morality, violence, politics, spirituality, or sexuality. Although interesting moral debates perennially appear in the media and academia concerning the appropriateness of games' ability to deal with such adult concepts, very little is known about the intersection between games, playfulness, and sexuality and what this might mean for players.

This book offers an in-depth, ethnographic look into the phenomenon of erotic role-play through the experiences of players in multiplayer and tabletop role-playing games. Brown explores why participants engage in erotic role-play, discusses the rules involved in erotic role-play, and uncovers what playing with sexuality in ludic environments means for players, their partners, and their everyday lives. Taken together, this book provides a rich, nuanced, and detailed account of a provocative topic.

Ashley ML Brown is a lecturer in digital games theory and design at Brunel University, London. She completed her PhD at the University of Manchester in sociology in autumn 2013. She volunteers as secretary for the Digital Games Research Association (DiGRA) and is a founding member of the recently created U.K. chapter of DiGRA.

Routledge Advances in Game Studies

Sexuality in Role-Playing Games

Ashley ML Brown

Routledge
Taylor & Francis Group

New York London

First published 2015
by Routledge
711 Third Avenue, New York, NY 10017

and by Routledge
2 Park Square, Milton Park, Abingdon, Oxon OX14 4RN

First issued in paperback 2017

Routledge is an imprint of the Taylor & Francis Group, an informa business

Library of Congress Cataloging-in-Publication Data

Brown, Ashley M. L., 1986–
Sexuality in role-playing games / by Ashley M.L. Brown.
    pages cm. — (Routledge advances in game studies ; 2)
Includes bibliographical references and index.
    1. Computer sex. 2. Fantasy games—Social aspects. 3. Role playing.
    4. Sexual fantasies. 5. Sex. I. Title.
HQ66.B76 2015
306.70285—dc23   2014041073

ISBN 13: 978-1-138-09770-4 (pbk)
ISBN 13: 978-1-138-81255-0 (hbk)

Typeset in Sabon
by codeMantra

This book is dedicated to the participants who made the research possible.

Contents

1 Finding the Erotic in Role-Play

My night elf's leather boots gave off a tinny, hollow echo as she ran beneath the tracks of the Deeprun Tram. Halfway between the human capital of Stormwind and the dwarven and gnomish capital of Ironforge, I had intentionally made her fall off one of the open tram cars. My intention was to explore the windowed sides of the underground transportation tunnel. I had read on a forum that if you went to the right spot at the right time and right angle, you could see one of two rare monsters: Nessie, a giant sea monster, or Maws, a giant shark. Jumping off the tram midway meant I would have a long and time-consuming run to get back to one of the capital cities, but that didn't concern me. It would be worth it to see pixelated renditions of the rare and hard to find underwater beasts.

As I made my blue-haired, purple-skinned elf run along, I kept my left mouse button firmly pressed, controlling the camera angle so I could sweep from side to side looking for Nessie and Maws. Concentrating on my task, I was startled when the chat window in the bottom left corner of my screen began to fill with text. My elf stopped running as I released the 'W' key. I had thought that, aside from the passengers in the whizzing tram cars overhead, I was completely alone in the underground tunnel. Sweeping the mouse from side to side, changing my view of the surrounding area, I saw the two characters responsible for this sudden outburst of activity: two dwarves. A male dwarf with a long, flame-coloured beard and thinning hair pressed a female dwarf with intricate braids coiled to either side of her head against the windows of the tunnel. With no witnesses, except perhaps Maws and Nessie, the couple disrobed. As the players clicked on their characters' armour and dragged the items into their inventory, the clothing began to disappear off the avatars. Although the two dwarves stood still, now in only their underwear, the players typed commands, also called emotes, which filled my screen. These commands indicated the two dwarves were lovingly caressing one another.

My elf stood only ten metres away, confused and unmoving. If it were possible to control facial expressions, I suspect she would have been as slack-jawed and open-mouthed as I was at at my desk. I tried to comprehend what I was seeing, but I was too startled to make much sense of it. My next reaction was one of embarrassment. Although the couple seemed not to have noticed my elf in the darkness of the tunnel, I felt ashamed. It was as though I had been caught peeping through a bedroom door as an intimate scene unfolded before my eyes. Immediately, I turned my elf around and ran back to Ironforge, trying to forget what I had witnessed.

But I could not forget. That first experience nine years ago made me curious. I wondered what could have brought the two dwarves together in that tunnel. I wondered what the sexual appeal of the game's highly stylised and cartoonish avatars could be, and I wondered what meanings, if any, these in-game interactions had for the people controlling the avatars. As I would learn through my experiences playing and some casual research on *World of Warcraft*'s (*WoW*) forums, what I had witnessed was erotic role-play, often abbreviated as ERP, and it was quite common. I learned the two dwarf players were using built-in game functions, such as the emote, to type actions for their characters. I learned this was often done to build a narrative and relationship between characters, to add an emotional depth to their individual legends. But I still had questions. I wondered if the fantastical nature of the game added something players felt was lacking in their out-of-game sexual repertoire; I wondered if there were rules and boundaries governing what is acceptable behaviour in erotic role-play; and I still wondered what meanings, if any, these interactions had for players.

As my interest in role-play as a pastime increased I began to play tabletop role-playing games such as *Dungeons and Dragons*. Much like my experiences in *World of Warcraft*, I noticed a wealth of sexual content present there as well. In addition to the often bawdy plots of the games I was involved in, I discovered role-playing guidebooks and handbooks with hundreds of rules to guide players in their inclusion of sexual content. I even found an entire book dedicated to providing players with background for how to incorporate erotic game-play into role-playing sessions, replete with detailed charts dictating which dice to roll to determine sexual performance or the likelihood of conception by pairings of various fantasy races. My interest in erotic role-play deepened and I began to think of the social connections and implications the activity might have for those who choose to play with it. My queries began to take an academic tone and my doctoral research project began to take shape.

This book emerged out of a research project spanning four years. Four years is not only a significant time commitment in terms of research scheduling but also in terms of life. It is therefore fair to say this book is a part of my life as much as it represents the lives and lived experiences of the participants with whom I spent so many hours. From buying corn-based snacks and rolling dice with the tabletop group to staying up until two in the morning collecting supplies for the *World of Warcraft* guild's weekly dungeon raid, this book represents the memories of not just my participants but also my own. Although not an autoethnography by any means, this book both begins and ends within my lived experience. More than just matching the chosen research methodology, detailed in some depth in Chapter Three, the deep commitment I feel towards my research and my participants is symbolic of what it means to role-play and to be a part of a role-playing community.

Perhaps the commitment is also symbolic of the topic matter at hand. Topics relating to sexuality and the erotic, as erotic role-play is, are usually entrenched within taboo. Those whose hobbies involve the erotic are often particularly open to misrepresentation or otherwise having their activities misread within a larger societal context of what constitutes 'normal' behaviour. Not only does this book contend with some of those stereotypes and prejudices head on but it also touches on the sense of community espoused by players involved in the activity. Much like hobbyists of any other category, the participants in this study formed a collective bond over a mutually shared interest. In addition to being an activity or hobby shared by participants, erotic role-play can also be defined in a multitude of ways, which will be discussed below.

DEFINING EROTIC ROLE-PLAY

Although an example was provided above in the case of the dwarves in the Deeprun Tram, erotic role-play can take many forms. From tabletop games and live action role-play to their digital counterparts, any type of role-play has the potential to become erotic. Taken at its loosest definition, erotic role-play is a form of role-playing that involves erotic themes. Dressing up in sexy costumes such as a police officer and a speeding driver to involve power scenarios in sexual play could be considered a type of erotic role-play, but this type of erotic play is not covered by the research presented here. Whilst erotic role-play's definition can be wide enough to encapsulate a variety of activities, it is used in this book in a very specific way. It is predominately used to reflect a participant-defined activity that involves the incorporation of sexual or erotic content into pre-existing role-play scenarios in digital or tabletop role-playing games. These games exist independently of the erotic content taking place. By this I mean that although probably the highlight of many players' in-game experience, they do not play the game solely for the purposes of ERP. This is perhaps the strongest way in which erotic role-play differs from other variants of sexual play such as dress up. Although an enjoyable aspect of the play experience to be sure, participants had other role-play and game goals they focused on in addition to erotic ones. From engaging in complex and demanding dungeon raids to politically manipulating non-player characters to fighting giant, scary werewolves, each of the players in this study participated in and enjoyed other aspects of the games they played.

Through research, I found other scholars had written, although sparsely, about erotic role-play in the past. However, as Chapter Two will demonstrate, these writings amount to a few pages or even a few paragraphs simply acknowledging the practice takes place. Some researchers have discussed other forms of online sexuality and these definitions will be used here to develop an understanding of what erotic role-play is and how it differs from virtual sex and cybersex.

For example, cybersex and virtual sex share similarities with erotic role-play online in that all use text as a way of communicating erotic actions. Just as the two dwarves in the Deeprun Tram filled my chat window with textual descriptions of their characters' actions through the use of the command/emote, virtual sex or cybersex in chatrooms are similarly text-based. However, there are many important differences in the definitions and functionalities of erotic role-play and other types of text-based erotic activity. Cybersex has been defined as "a social interaction between at least two persons who are exchanging real time digital messages in order to become sexually aroused and satisfied" (Döring 2004, p. 863). Likewise, past research into multi-user dungeons found "virtual sex ... consists of two or more players typing descriptions of physical actions, verbal statements, and emotional reactions for their characters" (Turkle 1995, p. 223). Whilst erotic role-play online does usually involve the real-time exchange of textual descriptions of physical actions and emotional reactions, and more often than not arousal and masturbation do occur, this is not true of all erotic role-play, particularly that which happens during in-the-flesh tabletop gaming. Additionally, these definitions focus only on the immediate act itself and ignore the larger significance the activity may have for the characters or players involved.

For many, erotic role-play is seen as contributing to a deeper narrative that is meaningful for both the player and their character. Such a narrative is cohesively built with respect to a game's overarching story and interactions with other player-characters and even non-player characters. To be consistent with the methodology of the book, described at length in Chapter Three, it is best to let the activity be described within the words of an erotic role-player. Penpy, a participant in the research informing this book, writes that erotic role-play is

> role-play of an erotic nature, but I would caution [those unfamiliar] to the difference between ERP and cybering [cybersex]. Cybering is the exchange of sexually suggestive sentences specifically to sexually excite the other person and yourself. ERP is more of a natural progression of a storyline between fictional characters.
>
> (Personal interview with Penpy, 2011)

Penpy's definition was echoed by the other participants. Rather than only being about arousal and virtual sex, they insisted erotic role-play is about narrative, story, relationships between characters, and play. Participant definitions of erotic role-play distinguish it from other forms of online or textual sexual play by highlighting the importance of story, diegetic believability, and staying in-character. Unlike virtual sex or cybersex, in which people describe sexual actions and reactions for themselves, erotic role-players describe sexual actions and reactions for their characters.

Whilst online sexuality has been studied in a variety of ways, erotic role-play has not. This is particularly true for erotic role-play that happens during in-the-flesh tabletop role-playing sessions. The use of the term 'in-the-flesh' may in itself be confusing, as surely all role-play occurring between humans by default must occur in-the-flesh of those participating. Even in online role-play, the acts of typing, moving the mouse, smiling, and experiencing play happens just as much in the physical body as it does on the screen. However, what I mean to say when I suggest tabletop role-playing occurs in-the-flesh is that all participants are physically present and co-located in the same physical and geographical location.

Defining tabletop erotic role-play by its physical location is useful for further developing a definition of the activity. There are other forms of co-located erotic role-play that occur in-the-flesh and that are separate to, and different from, the erotic role-play discussed in this book. Other researchers, for example, have looked at the Ars Amandi system for including sexual content into live action role-playing games (LARPs). Ars Amandi uses the hands and arms of consenting players, along with breathing and eye contact, to simulate intercourse. LARP researcher Lizzie Stark (2011) interviewed Emma Wieslander, the creator of Ars Amandi, for her blog and discussed the importance of having a system to simulate sexual interactions, especially when most gaming systems tend to focus exclusively on violence. Given the system is intended for LARP communities, Ars Amandi requires players to physically touch one another as they describe their character's actions. It is in this way that it differs significantly from tabletop, in-the-flesh role-play, which doesn't involve player touching.

Similarly, outside the boundaries of what might typically be thought of as games, dress-up sex and BDSM (bondage, domination, sado/masochistic) might be thought of as a type of role-play. In fact, despite the tendency to think of games, toys and play predominantly in terms of childhood activities, a variety of adult activities involve games, toys and playful types of sexuality. The costumes found year-round in adult shops are often thematically similar to those found around Halloween. The costumes often centre on roles or occupations that deliberately provoke a power dynamic, e.g. speeding driver and police officer, housekeeper and homeowner, nurse and doctor, student and teacher. These costumes invite their wearers to temporarily take on the role of the occupation or situation represented through their clothing. It is in this way that these costumes' function is similar to their Halloween counterparts. It encourages, or at least provides a medium, through which role-play can occur. On a basic level, such costumes upset or inflate the power dynamics present in a relationship by allowing their wearers to take on the role or persona represented by the costume. Once the costume is taken off and the session ends, the costume-based role-play ends and those playing the roles reassume their everyday identities.

The costuming and setting involved with BDSM play likewise invokes a play with power. From collars and leashes to furniture designed to look and function like a dungeon or torture chamber, the undercurrent of BDSM speaks to an imbalance of power. For the duration of a scene or session, practitioners undertake the role of a dominant or submissive, master or slave, top or bottom, or any combination therein for the purposes of erotic play, sensuality, fun, and sexual gratification. After the BDSM session is complete, participants return to their existing roles and the existing power structures between participants is also reasserted.

In both the cases of using costumes for erotic play and BDSM, the temporary undertaking of identities for the purposes of enjoyment can be thought of as a type of game. J. Tuomas Harviainen (2011) makes the argument that BDSM is a type of live action role-play and argues for its consideration as a type of game. To make this argument, Harviainen uses Bernard Suits' definition of a game, which states, "to play a game is to engage in activity directed towards bringing about a specific state of affairs, using only means permitted by rules, where the rules prohibit more efficient in favour of less efficient means, and where such rules are accepted just because they make possible such an activity" (2005, p. 49). In the case of BDSM and costumed sex, explicit or implicit rules govern the erotic play taking place that 'prohibit more efficient' means of having sex in favour of 'less efficient' means that increase the enjoyment of the activity. Such rules might encourage participants to remain talking and acting as their chosen role for the duration, or such rules might seek to prohibit sexual gratification for as long as possible so as to increase the enjoyment and duration of the act. Either way, scholars such as Harviainen argue through the presence of rules that sexual activities involving role-play are not only ludic but can also be considered a game.

In developing a definition of erotic role-play to be used throughout this book, it is important to take into consideration past research and philosophies on what can be considered a role-playing game. By virtue of the existence of rules and location within game worlds, erotic role-play should be considered either a part of larger games or a game in its own right. The argument can be made for games that explicitly include rules for sexuality, such as *Vampire: The Masquerade*, where erotic role-play is a part of the overall gaming experience. For other games that lack endogenic rules for playing with sexual content, such as *World of Warcraft*, erotic role-play may still be thought of as a game but a game the rules of which exist exogenously from the game's core content.

Likewise, it is important to note there are many forms of erotic role-play but this book speaks to one type in particular. Unlike costumed sex play, BDSM, LARP, or Ars Amandi, the erotic role-play discussed in this book does not involve physically, in-the-flesh touching other players. The erotic role-play discussed in this book involves many similar components to the types of role-play listed above, in that roles are undertaken, power dynamics shift, players take on rules to prohibit efficient sexual gratification (or sometimes any sexual gratification), and a fictional scene or scenario with erotic tones is played out, but never do the players touch, change their breathing, or necessarily make eye contact with other players. So using past research and informants' definitions, a succinct way to describe erotic role-play would be a scene or a session of a role-playing game that focuses on erotic themes and sexual actions for fun, diegetic consistency, or to develop the narrative of a character or characters and does not involve any physical, in-the-flesh touching between players.

OUTLINE OF THE BOOK

This book uses ethnographic methods to explore how erotic role-play is used in tabletop games and the massive multiplayer online role-playing game *World of Warcraft*, with careful attention paid to the nuanced meanings given to it by players. As the book will go on to elaborate, erotic role-play was found to provide players with alternate ways to express and experience sexuality through fantastical themes and environments removed from mundane, everyday life. The primary research question, which asks if erotic role-players experiment with non-normative sexuality in their role-play and if so, how, was answered through a thematic analysis of focus-group and interview responses with groups of erotic role-players. The resulting analysis found erotic role-players do incorporate sexual themes and acts that are different from their sexual routine and do so in a nuanced way.

I have analysed participant responses in three key ways. The first uses Erving Goffman's frame analysis (1974) to interpret the oscillating frames of experience that occur during erotic role-play as different from the frames involved during out-of-game sexual behaviour. In analysing the data in such a way, it becomes clear sexualities outside of the participants' normative routine can enter game play through the distancing between the diegetic framework of characters interacting in a fantasy world and participants' out-of-character primary social framework. The second utilises the largely neglected but well-established theories of games and play, alongside Foucault's (1984) theories of the care of the self, to examine how rules helped ensure erotic role-play stayed within the diegetic frame of experience and alternate ways of viewing sexual normativity occurred within multiple frames outside of the primary social framework.

Theories on games and play have recently experienced a revival in interest with the advent of computer games and the popularity of the academic field of games studies. These theories understand play as a frivolous and voluntary activity (Huizinga, 1949) that seeks to explore mysteries (Caillois, 1961), so erotic role-play can be understood as an activity undertaken voluntarily to explore the mysteries of sexuality with the reassurance the activity is frivolous and thus contains limited risks to the self. Rules are additionally understood as confining potential self-discoveries made through erotic role-play and limiting their potential to supplant normative notions of 'austere' sexuality (Foucault, 1978) with alternate sexualities developed through play. Finally, the potential crossover effects between in-game and out-of-game are analysed with frame analysis (Goffman, 1974) and the sociology of friendship to understand the functionality and meaning participants place on their in-game interactions. In reading interview responses about the relationships developed through erotic role-play as a type of performance of friendship, another layer of emotionality is added to the description of erotic role-play. In assessing the phenomenon in such a way, the sociological significance of erotic role-play emerges in its ability to redefine embodied sexuality and upset binary assumptions of what constitutes 'real' and 'virtual' sexuality and the differences between online and offline interactions.

SEX, GAMES, AND SEX GAMES

The second chapter of this book explores what is currently known about the topics of sexuality and gaming. In order to further differentiate and define erotic role-play, the chapter begins by pointing out sexual content in games, although controversial in recent years, has likely always been a part of human play practices. Using examples of offline party games such as 'Spin the Bottle' and 'Seven Minutes in Heaven', the chapter demonstrates that playing with sexual themes exists in other past times and cultural artefacts besides role-playing games. Following the works of Michel Foucault (1978; 1984), normative sexuality is defined in this chapter for use throughout the book as a subjective relationship between individuals and an ethical code that prioritises and values certain expressions of sexuality over others. Discourse is defined as the language of institutional power that enforces ethical codes and delineates that which is normative. To put it simply, normativity in this book reflects the routine sexual behaviours in participants' 'real', everyday, out-of-game lives. The chapter then highlights some theoretical underpinnings that highlight the importance of sexual play in defining games and play overall, and the overall meanings sexual play and play in virtual worlds might have for identity work and conceptions of self.

The final section of this chapter highlights recent research concerning problematic sexual content in games and the relationship this research has to the review and ratings of games.

EROTIC ROLE-PLAYERS

After defining what erotic role-play is and what has been written surrounding similar topics, the third chapter investigates who erotic role-plays.

Because erotic role-players are a hard-to-reach population, given taboos surrounding sexuality in Western culture and other reasons mentioned in this chapter, very little is known about the general population of players. Existing demographic data about MMO (massively multiplayer online game) players and role-players more generally is presented here to try to gain some insight about the population under discussion. Demographic information about the participants who took part in the study informing this book are also presented here, along with information about the methodology used. Unlike texts or films, which can be critically read and combined with audience studies, role-playing games need to be experienced as virtual worlds. This chapter outlines the epistemological considerations that shaped how the research was conducted and how data was gathered for research. This chapter outlines the importance of experiential knowledge of both participants and researcher as a form of data.

MULTIPLE FRAMES

Chapter Four seeks to answer the primary research question: Do erotic role-players experiment with non-normative sexuality in their role-play and if so, how? The chapter answers the research question through the use of interview and focus-group responses from participants that show erotic role-players do indeed experiment with sexuality in their role-play and they do so in nuanced ways. Further elaboration illustrates there are few similarities between players' sexuality and that of their characters, which is interpreted through frame analysis to highlight erotic role-play's existence within a bounded space. A distinction is made between in-game (diegetic) activities and out-of-game behaviours, which occur in the primary social frame. Within this distinction, the affordance erotic role-play makes to the ability to safely explore emotional connections and sexual activities through the frivolity of play and, for the *World of Warcraft* participants, anonymity will be explored. The tenuous interplay between fantasy worlds, wherein almost anything is possible, and the ludicity of erotic role-play, wherein everything is playful, is explored as a potential contributor to a unique discourse of sexuality for participants.

THE ROLE OF RULES

Chapter Five explores the use of rules to include and exclude sexual themes from erotic role-play. The chapter looks at not just officially published rules included as part of a game (endogenous), or social rules found in *World of Warcraft's* Terms of Use to govern acceptable player behaviour (exogenous), or even social rules within the game world to dictate appropriate character behaviour (diegetic) but also rules players created themselves.

The role of rules in erotic role-play is read within a larger social context of sexual normativity. In this way, rules are seen as dictating not only the social appropriateness of including sexuality in games but also the outside effects this inclusion may have. Rules that seek to limit the crossover between the diegetic experiences of characters and the social 'reality' of players are explored for potential contributions to an understanding of the functionality of sexual normativity within and outside of erotic role-play.

ERP IRL

Chapter Six focuses on data-analysis and relies heavily on original data of the research to challenge stereotypes of erotic role-players and binary assumptions about 'virtual' and 'real' sexuality. In exploring how content in the game crossed over into participants' 'real' lives, several commonly held perceptions about who erotic role-plays and why they do so are called into question. More than just for carnal, in-the-flesh pleasure, although that did sometimes occur, erotic role-play was most commonly associated with multiple, non-sexual pleasures such as creative expression or the development of friendships. Through the findings of this chapter, a nuanced view of erotic role-play and its effect on participants' lives is provided through an account of their experiences.

THE FUTURE OF EROTIC ROLE-PLAY

Chapter Seven reviews the results of the data. Whether or not erotic role-play is used to explore non-normative sexuality, what effect game rules have on erotic play, and what crossover, if any, occurs between the game world and participants' everyday lives are considered. Through an exploration of the major findings of the research, several previously unexamined stereotypes of erotic role-players are addressed. In examining these stereotypes and the counter-evidence found in the data, an accurate picture of the participants in this study and their motivations to erotic role-play are provided. In challenging stereotypes and presenting an accurate representation of both the phenomenon and the population of erotic role-players, groundwork is laid for future research on erotic role-play and sexuality in games. But of course, games and player populations do not exist in stasis. The end of this chapter highlights how some recently released role-playing games have dealt with erotic role-play. Through using examples such as The Elder Scrolls Online, speculation is given that online games will become increasingly open to 'adult' sexual content in the future as research, like that contained within this book, demonstrates adult players want, and will go to great lengths to include, sexual content in their games.

2   Sex, Games, and Sex Games

Although the research that informs this book focuses on a relatively new way of playing with sexuality, sex has always been a topic for play. Offline games that focus on aspects of sexuality or engage directly with sexual themes have likely always existed, even if documentation of such games has not. Examples of such games include party games like Spin the Bottle and Seven Minutes in Heaven.

A game such as Spin the Bottle, typically played at house parties by adolescents sitting in a circle with a bottle in the centre, contains hints of eroticism as players kiss whomever the bottle points to at the end of its spin. In a more explicit variation of this classic game, entitled Seven Minutes in Heaven,[1] players selected by spinning a bottle go into a dark, enclosed space within a home and spend seven minutes kissing, caressing, or partaking in other erotic activities. Similarly, there exists a growing market for card and board games at sex shops that encourage lovers to roll dice or draw cards that correspond to sexual interactions and body parts. Interestingly, these games are usually found shelved near toys and costumes that are also suitably marked out for use in adult play. Costumes have a particular connection to role-play and will be discussed at some length later in this chapter.

As the above description of the organisation of games, toys, and dress-up costumes at sex shops highlights, play and sexuality have a unique relationship. In most aspects of everyday life, this relationship goes unacknowledged. It is very unlikely, for example, that any major international toy shop would carry adult toys, games, or costumes. Even if the adult items are made from similar materials (card stock, dice, cloth) and intended for a similar outcome (fun, enjoyment, social bonding), they are still placed in a separate market. To even suggest a chain toy store should carry items intended for sexual use is an uncomfortable prospect.

The relationship between sex and play is one which is conflicted. Although we know sex toys and erotic games exist and, to some degree, we are growing to accept playful behaviours from adults, there remains an uneasy tension surrounding what can and should be made available for play. The following pages of this chapter aim to highlight and describe this tension by first focusing on the theoretical relationship between sex, play, and games. Interestingly enough, many philosophical definitions of play and games use sex as an example to define the boundaries of what may be considered ludic. Such writings will be considered before moving on to discuss examples of how sex and sexualities have been represented in popular games. Here, tension is punctuated by concerns over morality and ethics, sometimes gaining enough momentum to provoke a moral panic. Finally, this chapter will conclude by describing how these tensions relate to the main topic of the book: erotic role-play.

Tension exists between erotic role-play and other traditional forms of play in that erotic role-play usually takes place outside the bedroom. This occurs both in the sense that role-playing is a social activity done with multiple others with varying degrees of intimacy and in the sense that, diegetically speaking, erotic role-play often takes place in public settings. Moral and ethical tension exists when the activity takes place in an environment that is available to people of all ages, including children. Game worlds suddenly become a contested territory wherein the appropriateness of content available for play becomes subject to the moral stance of the players. Each of these sections represents key ways we can think about sex, games, and sex games.

PHILOSOPHY, PLAY, AND SEX

Some of the earliest writings within the study of games and play discuss sexuality. Usually these discussions are undertaken in an attempt to define the act of play and the nature of games. In an early example, Georges Bataille (1952) mentions the alternative moralities present in gameplay as forming a type of allegory for erotic transgression. Bataille's writing on eroticism is the earliest known example of a scholarly work that connects games, play, and sexuality. It is therefore interesting that from the outset, the tension between play and sexuality is highlighted through discussions of morality. Similarly, Roger Caillois (1961) wrote about play's ability to transgress secret or mysterious topics and make even the darkest aspects of society available for play. He writes, "Without a doubt, secrecy, mystery, and even travesty can be transformed into play activity, but it must be immediately pointed out that this transformation is necessarily to the detriment of the secret and mysterious, which play exposes, publishes, and somehow expends" (Caillois 1961, p. 4). Like Bataille, although not as explicit, Caillois recognises play's power to transform ordinarily mysterious or secret topics and activities into playful ones. Caillois also notes, however, the very act of making them playful expends all that is secret or mysterious about the topics or activities. To play with sex, which is arguably secret and mysterious, is to expend the secrecy and mystery of the act.

In addition to being used to define some aspect of play, sex has also been used to reach a definition of games. Bernard Suits uses sexuality as a foil for defining games by tightening his definition of what games are to exclude sexual activities. At one point he goes as far as to plainly state, "Playing games is different from sexual activity. ..." (Suits 2005 [1978], p. 83). In the book, he eventually comes to the conclusion that sex cannot be considered a game because "losing the game implies that someone else has won the game, whereas failing to complete the sexual act does not imply a winner" (Suits 1978, p. 83). Suits uses sexual acts to further his definition of what games are by examining the conditions for both winning and losing a game. If achieving orgasm may be considered 'completing' a sex act and 'winning' at sex, then failure to reach orgasm means the game is left incomplete. Failure to reach orgasm does not, however, mean one or more players have lost. Just as an outdoor game might be postponed due to inclement weather or the discovery of a cheat might mean a game is restarted, Suits points out there are many conditions in which games may end without completion but to be considered a game, a loss must be achieved. Although a lack of orgasm may result in disappointment, it does not result in losing the game. The problem of considering sexual acts as games, for Suits, lies within orgasm's dual responsibilities as goal and completion. If, however, the sexual activity does not centre orgasm as its goal, it then becomes possible for that activity to be considered a game.

Building on the above examples, other writers have commented on how sex, an activity usually coded as adult, can allow for the emergence of playful behaviours that would otherwise be coded as childish. The argument will be made here that the act of playing with erotic and sexual themes is one way in which difficult, uncomfortable, or embarrassing ideas and activities can be explored. The connection between the concept of play, which nearly always refers to child-like behaviour, to one of eroticism and adult sexual activity is often a difficult one to make, due to the normative construction of sexuality within our primary moral and ethical frameworks, but there is evidence that suggests play is a regular function of romantic adult relationships. Brian Sutton-Smith noted that often adults play "with each other in innumerable ways, painting each other's bodies, eating food off of each other, playing hide the thimble with bodily crevices, communicating in public with their own esoteric vocabulary, and, in general teasing and testing each other with playful impropriety" (Sutton-Smith 2001, p. 3). The activities highlighted by Sutton-Smith are often taken for granted as flirtatious behaviour, but he does well to point out their playful nature. The element of play that governs and directs flirtatious behaviour allows space for impropriety or otherwise norm-transgressive acts to emerge. Likewise, medical doctor and relationship therapist William Betcher notes:

> Sex is the last great preserve of adult play, where even the dourest pillars of our community are permitted to whisper sweet nothings. If I were to urge you to do but one thing in trying to improve your sex life, it would be: don't turn it into work.
>
> (Betcher 1987, p. 111)

In this quote, Betcher not only contrasts work and play but also makes reference to play's existence outside of sexual normativity. Although there are many ways to define sexual normativity, I rely on Foucault (1984) to define it as an individual's mode of subjection to, and interpretation of, the ethical codes that dictate 'healthy' behaviour, usually through a renunciation of the self and a mastery of desire. By writing that in play, even 'the dourest pillars of our community are permitted to whisper sweet nothings', Betcher notes that play becomes a means by which adults can loosen the attachment between their sense of self and ethical codes relating to sexuality with a minimal risk to the effects this has on their ethical self-constitution.

In such a view, play becomes a bounded space. I use the term 'bounded space' as a way of referencing and encompassing the affordances play offers to the exploration of sexual themes and topics. In this sense, bounded space is metaphor that encompasses both the idea of the alternate realities entered into during play as well as play's separation from normative ethical subject-constitution. In another founding definition of play, Johan Huizinga writes that play "proceeds within its own proper boundaries of time and space according to fixed rules and in an orderly manner" (1949, p. 13). Taking from Huizinga the idea that play is bound both by the time it takes for the play activity to be accomplished as well as the space required for the activity, this book as a whole endeavours to elaborate on the ethical codes present in play. This will be accomplished through a detailing of the 'fixed rules' mentioned in Huizinga's quote. Rules are not only a defining feature of games but also a ludic mechanic that makes possible alternate ethical subject-constitution through its function as ethical codes.

The primary way games are distinguished from play is through the use of rules. Whilst play can be, and often is, a free-form activity, games are bound by rules. Rules outline acceptable and unacceptable behaviour in a way that is conducive to reaching a defined goal. However, games must be further defined to take into account their place in alternate realities and the ways in which they foster the creation and application of alternate ethical codes. Role-playing has often been absent from literature seeking to define games as it is often viewed as lacking fixed and stable rules, but it is important to consider the ways in which role-playing can be defined here as this book focuses on erotic role-playing. Rather than discussed as a game, role-play is more often discussed as play, storytelling, or mimicry. Caillois, for example, can be said to include role-play in his definition of games only insofar as it is a form of mimicry (1961). However, his definition of mimicry follows most closely other definitions of play and not games. In his attempt to classify types of games, Caillois writes, "Play can consist not only of deploying actions or submitting one's fate in an imaginary milieu, but of becoming an illusory character oneself, and of so behaving" (1961, p. 19). Although this definition describes an aspect of role-playing, it does not describe the structure of role-playing games and lacks an emphasis on rules.

One definition of games that has been used by some scholars of role-play (e.g. Harviainen 2012) is the one developed by Bernard Suits. 'His definition is broad enough to take into account the role of rules in behaviour similar to mimicry. Suits writes, "To play a game is to engage in activity directed towards bringing about a specific state of affairs, using only means permitted by rules, where the rules prohibit more efficient in favour of less efficient means, and where such rules are accepted just because they make possible such an activity" (2005, p. 49). To use a more basic and familiar game as an example, the specific state of affairs that forms the end goal of football would be to score the most points by repeatedly crossing an arbitrary line with a ball. This goal could easily be achieved by picking up the ball and carrying it over the line. It is the rules, however, that state the line needs to be placed in a specific location, have specific dimensions, be defended by opposing players, and the ball must not be touched by certain players' hands, which increase the difficulty, and enjoyment, of the sport and also make it a game.

Now that an understanding of what constitutes a game has been established, erotic role-playing must be shown to fit the definition of a game in order to more thoroughly assess how it, along with play, allows for the temporary subjectivisation of players to new ethical codes (rules). To do this, Suits' definition of games will be slightly modified to establish erotic role-play's reliance on rules. To play an erotic role-playing game, then, is to bring about a specific state of affairs or reach an end goal using only the means permitted by rules or the game master, where the rules and game master prohibit more efficient in favour of less efficient means and where such rules are accepted just because they make erotic role-playing possible. Such a definition not only establishes erotic role-play as an activity removed from sexual behaviour but also illuminates the role of rules as a type of ethical code. Rather than understanding erotic role-play as a virtual environment in which any sexual behaviour is allowed, rules exist to shape behaviour and make it ludic. Whether the goal be an in-the-flesh orgasm or the development of a narrative between characters, rules function to provide a code of behaviour for players and their characters. Therefore, there is reason to believe that when entering erotic role-play in a game, players and their characters subject themselves to the ethical code present in the rules of a given game.

To elaborate on how rules form a type of ethical code for the emergence of sexuality in games, the rules themselves need to be broken down to account for the multiple frames through which a game is experienced. During a role-play session, there are at least three sets of rules governing play. Markus Montola (2008) combines Gary Alan Fine's (1983) three frames with Björk and Holopainen's (2003) division of exogenous and endogenous rules to create a depth of understanding about the rule processes involved in role-playing. These divisions of how rules are experienced and involved in play rely on the understanding that reality is experienced through frames.

The idea of frames, developed by Erving Goffman (1974), allows us to think about play and games as activities separate from everyday behaviour. Every player experiences the primary social framework that, as defined by Goffman, is representative of individual conceptualisation and synthesis of experience in the real world. Goffman writes, "The primary frameworks of a particular social group constitute a central element of its culture, especially insofar as understandings emerge concerning principal classes of schemata, the relations of these classes to one another, and the sum total of forces and agents that these interpretive designs acknowledge to be loose in the world. One must try to form an image of a group's framework of frameworks- its belief system, its 'cosmology'. ..." (Goffman 1974, p. 27). The primary social framework therefore makes reference to and engages with some notion of players' everyday, mundane lives outside the games they play.

When they sit down to play a game, however, there are at least two more frames to be 'keyed' into. According to Goffman, keying refers to "the set of conventions by which a given activity, one already meaningful in terms of some primary framework, is transformed into something patterned on this activity but seen by the participants to be something quite else" (1974, pp. 43–44). The example Goffman uses to illustrate this idea of keying comes from watching animals play. He notes the play of animals, from otters to monkeys, is based on the already known and defined behaviour of fighting. Many of the behaviours associated with fighting, such as physically violent gestures, are present in animals' play. However, the differences between fighting and playing are obvious.

Goffman notes that while "bitinglike behaviour occurs, no one is seriously bitten" (1974, p. 41). It is in this observation of the transformation of outward gestures of a behaviour associated with fighting in the primary framework that another framework is required to account for the interpretation of the actions as not serious or playful. By keying 'bitinglike' actions as playful, play itself is abstracted from the framework of routine behaviour and placed in a different category. Just as violent acts, which may ordinarily be at conflict with an individual's conception of an ethical self are excused when keyed as playful, so too might sexual acts. The keying of a situation as playful and the ensuing shift of frames plant playful acts within alternate perceptions and alternate realities, which allow for it to be read within alternate subjectivities. This is particularly true if the keyed act adheres to the ethical codes present in alternate realities.

Working from this idea that play is different from everyday behaviour, Gary Alan Fine built a secondary framework to simultaneously account for play's segregation from the everyday and to provide a way to study the specific level of interaction present in tabletop role-playing. The secondary framework, or the player frame, encompasses players' knowledge of the rules, mechanics, story, and other nuances of the game being played. In his words, players "manipulate their characters, having knowledge of the structure of the game, and having approximately the same knowledge that other players have. Players do not operate in light of their primary frameworks in terms of what is physically possible but in light of the conventions of the game" (Fine 1983, p. 186). The idea of a secondary player frame illuminates a switch in the active knowledges and behaviours employed during the activity. Rather than be limited by what is possible in the real world or primary framework, players choose their actions based on a specific knowledge relevant only to the game and their understanding of it. In doing so, players can be said to create "a subject connected to the rules of a game" (Sicart 2009, p. 63).

Where the primary framework focused on the player's everyday knowledge and the secondary framework focused on the player's knowledge as specific to the game, the tertiary framework focuses on character knowledge. In his ethnography on tabletop gaming, Gary Alan Fine noted the "gaming world is keyed in that the players not only manipulate characters; they are characters. The character identity is separate from the player identity" (1983, p. 186). Through Fine's observations, it is made clear that player and character identities are as separate as the realities each inhabit. Although all players manipulate their characters to perform actions within the game world and are in some ways the masters of that character's fate, role-players actively engage with a framework embedded in their character. The process of role-playing requires engagement with a character's primary framework by speaking and acting with the argot and knowledge of that character. Borrowing from literature and theatre studies, Markus Montola (2008) uses the term 'diegetic' to help summarise the ideas present in the tertiary framework and to encompass the storytelling elements present in role-playing. Montola additionally combined existing theory and summarised the frames experienced by role-players during play. In Montola's combination, three types of rules emerge, exogenous, endogenous, and diegetic. He illustrates each in the following:

- "Do not discuss non-game business during the game": exogenous.
- "A sword does d10 points of damage": endogenous.
- "Carrying a sword within the city limits is punishable by fine": diegetic.
  (Montola 2008, p. 23)

Exogenous in this case refers to players' self-created 'house rules' (Björk and Holopainen 2003). These are rules that are not stated explicitly in the game and are thus not always central to game play or even enforceable. For erotic role-play, house rules could take the form of a type of ethical code centred on the behaviour of players. Just as Montola gives the example of keeping conversations relevant to the game, an exogenous rule for erotic role-play might concern expectations of player behaviour. Such a rule might ask players to refrain from making jokes or innuendos during erotic scenes, for example. Such rules temporarily alter the ethical codes an individual subjects themselves to upon entering a game. Following Foucault, I suggest this in turn effects how the players conceive themselves as ethical subjects in their choice to abide, or not abide, by these rules.

Relying on Costikyan (2002), Björk and Holopainen (2003) define endogenous rules within the context of games' ability to create their own meanings. Such rules, which may also be termed mechanical or ludic, make reference to possible actions and the results of such actions within the game world. Here too players temporarily subject themselves and their characters to an alternate ethical code. For the purposes of erotic role-play, this may be viewed within the player frame as a type of discourse. Players might know that within a particular game world, sexually transmitted infections are present as a ludic mechanic that causes an infected character to take damage over time. They may wish to avoid such a hindrance and thus have their character abstain from unprotected sex. Such an endogenous rule thus functions in a similar way to Foucault's (1984) discourse. Just as individuals may internalise discourses that warn of the potential negative health effects of sexuality on the body, and thus construct a sexual regimen that considers the care of the self, players similarly respond on behalf of their characters. Through endogenous rules, players subjectivise themselves to the ethical codes of the game and develop an ethical sense of self through possible actions and their possible consequences.

Finally, diegetic rules make reference to the social rules that exist within a game world. Similar to endogenous rules, diegetic rules present a type of discourse. An example of such might be that within a given game world, certain types of characters, such as members of a religious order, are forbidden from sexual activities. Such rules, however, exist within the diegetic frame of experience. As the characters experience and come to know the game world and the ethical codes within it, they subject themselves to ethical codes that shape their development of an ethical self. Of course the player, as controller of the character, experiences this too through the oscillation of frames (Goffman 1974). The diegetic frame accounts for such a player experience and allows for the development of a temporary ethical self based on the ethics of the game world.

Diegetic rules and the diegetic frame are of particular importance in understanding erotic role-play as opening sexuality to play as it simultaneously provides limitations to character actions through discourse. Within such rules, that which is undesirable or indefensible within the normative ethics of reality can be engaged with through the employment of a game world's discourse. Within the diegetic, players are distanced, but not removed completely, from their own primary frameworks that dictate the normative sexual ethics that affect their everyday lives and sense of self. This slight distance, combined with the frivolous nature of play, theoretically causes the game-space to become an environment of manageable risk for the players to experiment with activities that would be considered in conflict with the ethical self in their primary framework. Whatever ideas, opinions, or activities are expressed in the diegetic largely remain there, giving players recourse to explain their actions. If taken to task in the primary framework outside the game about a violation of normative sexual ethics that occurred inside the game, players can claim a level of distance by right of play. "It was only a game" or "I was just following the rules" can be uttered in defence of an act that may have justification in the diegetic world but be seen as abhorrent in the real world.

Now that basic philosophical aspects of play have been discussed with regards to erotic role-play, it is important to define what is meant by sexual normativity. In order to understand how erotic role-play might challenge sexual normativity, a definition must be developed that understands human sexuality as an economy of pleasures, a transfer point for power and knowledge, and a historical repertoire of actions concerned with the subjective development of the self. Even a basic definition of sex as a physical act must take into consideration that it is more than a natural function of biology and reproduction. This troubles the ways in which certain acts might be defined as normative. For Foucault, sexuality "is the name that can be given to a historical construct: not a furtive reality that is difficult to grasp, but a great surface network in which the stimulation of bodies, the intensification of pleasures, the incitement to discourse, the formation of special knowledges, the strengthening of controls and resistances are linked to one another in accordance with a few major strategies of knowledge and power" (1978, p. 107). From Foucault's definition of sexuality, it becomes clear a definition of normative sexuality must take into account that the nature of the act is more than just a function of biological desires and is in fact historically constructed and the product of networks of knowledge and power.

The consideration of historical constructions of normative sexuality is of particular interest when attempting to locate erotic role-play as oppositional or at least existing outside normative sexuality. In his historical account, Foucault notes large general shifts in social and cultural policies and practices regarding sexuality and reads them as having originated in modes of ethical subjectivisation. He develops the term 'care of the self' to account for general changes in views of sexuality between the classical and imperial eras (O'Leary, 2002), and finds sexual behaviours "will derive from a profoundly altered ethics and from a different way of constituting oneself as the ethical subject of one's sexual behaviour" (Foucault 1984, p. 240). Specifically, Foucault accounts for a class change in the application of sexual ethics. Once demanded only of people with high social or political status, the universal principals of reason and nature found in the imperial era required everyone subject themselves to a 'certain art of living' (O'Leary 2002, p. 73). The art of living represents a type of sexual ethics, an economy of pleasure that emphasises the effects on the self. In the imperialist era, "the art of the self no longer focuses so much on the excesses that one can indulge in and that need to be mastered in order to exercise one's domination over others. It gives increasing emphasis to the frailty of the individual faced with the manifold ills that sexual activity can give rise to" (Foucault 1984, p. 238). For

Foucault, this change in sexual ethics comes along with a change in sexual behaviour. To give an example of this, Foucault writes about the changes in marital law from the classic to the imperial eras and notes a change in the relations to others impacts the change on the relations to the self.

> These developments may very well have occasioned, not a withdrawal into the self, but a new way of conceiving oneself in relation to one's wife, to others, to events, and to civic and political activities and a different way of considering oneself as the subject of one's pleasures. Hence the cultivation of the self would not be the necessary 'consequence' of these social modifications; it would not be their expression in the sphere of ideology, rather it would constitute an original response to them, in the form of a new stylistics of existence.
>
> (Foucault 1984, p.71)

The shift in the concerns of sexual ethics, from excess and domination to anxiety and austerity from the perceived ills derived from sexual acts, represents a change in ethical subjectivisation rather than an ethical code. In his analysis of Foucault's works on sexuality, Timothy O'Leary (2002) comments that although the changes in attitudes towards sex, ethics, and behaviour between the classical and imperial eras might be observed in Augustus' attempts to control marriage through law, Foucault believed the changes were better explained by a shift in ethical subject constitution. The importance placed on relations to the self as an ethical subject were universalised and sex became something that must be managed in order to remain consistent with health. The effects of passions, on the self and on the body, needed to be monitored so "its effects and disturbing consequences" along with its "many connections to disease and with evil" (Foucault 1984, p. 238) could be managed. This idea of managing the effects of sexuality on the body and on the self leads towards sexual practice that is subordinate to, or a part of, a normative regime of sexuality.

For erotic role-play and the question of whether or not it provides an outlet for non-normative sexual practice, however, a more thorough understanding of what is meant by normativity is needed. Rather than suggesting normativity can be defined as either the classical art of the self, which can be characterised by indulgence and domination, or imperial austerity and anxiety, normativity will be used to signify individual, ethical subjectivisation. To use the words of Foucault, I take normativity to mean "a mode of subjection in the form of obedience to a general law that is at the same time the will of a personal god; a type of work on oneself that implies a decipherment of the soul and a purificatory hermeneutics of the desires, and a mode of ethical fulfilment that tends toward self-renunciation" (1984, p. 240). Sexual normativity, then, is not only the moral codes and laws to which an individual is subjected but also how an individual interprets those codes and laws alongside their desires and their development of an ethical self.

In defining normativity as such, allowances are made for religious, ethical, and legal codes to which individual participants may be subjected, but the emphasis remains on the participants' relation to themselves. Such a definition allows the book to focus on how erotic role-players make sense of themselves, their characters, and their erotic role-play as ethical subjects in and outside game worlds. This is of particular importance as game worlds often have different ethical and legal codes than the real world and should be assessed accordingly. Additionally, such a definition takes into consideration virtuality's minimised presence on the body, in that many risks to physical health, such as disease, are minimised in erotic role-play's location within the virtual.

In understanding sexual normativity as the manifestation of ethical codes on the self, a definition must also be provided for discourse and its effects on the ethical subject. Discourse can generally be defined as the language of institutional power. Sexual discourse, then, constitutes the ways in which sex and sexuality are spoken about, not only in terms of context and content but also who does the speaking and where. In the introduction to *The History of Sexuality: Volume One*, Foucault defines sexual discourse in some depth. He writes:

> The central issue, then (at least in the first instance), is not to determine whether one says yes or no to sex, whether one formulates prohibitions or permissions, whether one asserts its importance or denies its effects, or whether one refines the words one uses to designate it; but to account for the fact that it is spoken about, to discover who does the speaking, the positions and viewpoints from which they speak, the institutions which prompt people to speak about it and which store and distribute the things that are said. … it permeates in order to reach the most tenuous and individual modes of behaviour, the paths that give it access to the rare or scarcely perceivable forms of desire … it penetrates and controls everyday pleasure.
>
> (1978, p. 11)

More than just language or speech, discourse is the dissemination of knowledge and power that shapes how individuals view themselves as ethical subjects. Both the art of living and the care of the self are informed by institutional discourses that seek to monitor sexuality and its effects on the body. As Foucault writes, discourse has the power to influence behaviour and control 'everyday pleasure.' Discourse provides the ethical, legal, and religious codes through which individuals develop their ethical sense of self and come to view themselves as ethical beings in their relationships to others.

In the real world, discourse takes the form of the power and knowledge that make up ethical codes of conduct, but in the virtual game world, discourse takes the form of rules. In games, rules take on multiple formats and multiple responsibilities but they are understood here as providing a type of discourse. Rules become a type of ethical code, dictating which actions are possible, if not socially acceptable, within a game world setting. In understanding rules as a type of discourse, erotic role-play becomes an interesting site for study as players and their characters are subjected to at least two types of sexual discourse at any given moment: that of the real world and that of the game world. These discourses may share similarities and may cross over, but each is unique in that actions considered ethically indefensible in the real world may be defendable within a game world. Previous analysis of the ethics at play in games such as *Grand Theft Auto* has found, for example, that players of the game develop a subject constitution that views their character's actions as defensible within the ethical frame of the game world (Juul 2005; Sicart 2009). That which is possible or even encouraged in games, such as killing police, is indefensible in-the-flesh and previous research has found players understand this and are able to separate the ethics of the game world from those of the real world. Understanding discourse in this way creates interesting insight into how players understand themselves as subjects of sexual ethics.

Increased use of technology, especially for recreation and play as in the *Grand Theft Auto* example, has significant implications for how we envision ourselves and our role in society. The advent of computer-mediated communication shaped relationality between the self and others by changing perceptions of the world. As Mark Poster wrote, "Subject constitution in the second media age occurs with the mechanism of interactivity" (1995, p. 33). Poster positions the move from watching or reading media to interacting with it within a cultural history. He contrasts the differences between the stability of modernity, as inherited through rationality and capitalism, and the uncertainty of postmodernity as evidenced by utopian dreams of technology. He writes:

> If modern society may be said to foster an individual who is rational, autonomous, centred, and stable (the "reasonable man" of the law, the educated citizen of representative democracy, the calculating "economic man" of capitalism, the grade-defined student of public education), then perhaps a postmodern society is emerging which nurtures forms of identity, different from, even opposite to, those of modernity.
> (1995, p. 24)

Poster frames the switch from modernity to postmodernity within the language of a technological change. He argues that if a postmodern society is emerging, it is emerging due to a change in the way information is exchanged. In his work on the second age of media, he posits technology is emerging as a medium for the creation of a new form of individual identity that may even be opposite to the identities constructed under modernity. He writes, "For what is at stake in these technical innovations, I contend, is not simply an increased 'efficiency' of interchange, enabling new avenues of investment, increased productivity at work and new domains of leisure and consumption, but a broad and extensive change in the culture, in the way identities are structured" (1995, p. 24). The idea that a change in medium of communication changes the ways in which identities are structured is of the utmost importance to erotic role-play. If it holds true that the medium changes relationalities to the self and others, then it may be assumed the movement of sexual activity from in-the-flesh acts to virtual or imagined acts would likewise influence the creation of a sexual self. In order to elaborate on how the creation of a virtual sexual self may be achieved, it is important to understand the idea that virtual reality consists of multiple alternate realities. To explain this, Poster gives the examples of how technological changes in the production of various forms of media have contributed to the idea that it is possible for multiple realities to exist.

Poster cites the development of the term 'real time' in the audio-production industry as evidence of how technology upsets traditional understandings of time. Real time describes recording a sound as it is listened to rather than looping and repeating a previously recorded sound. The modernist notion of time as stable and linear is upset by technology, which allows for the looping of past recordings into future productions. Such uses of technology, Poster argues, upset modernist ideas of how the world functions and allows for the development of a postmodern conception of reality as multiple. He goes on to link this idea to virtual reality and how an increasingly simulational culture transforms the identity of "originals and referentialities" (1995, p. 30).

> While still in their infancy, virtual reality programs attest to the increasing 'duplication', if I may use this term, of reality by technology. But the duplication incurs an alternation: virtual realities are fanciful imaginings that, in their difference from real reality, evoke play and discovery, instituting a new level of imagination. Virtual reality takes the imaginary of the word and the imaginary of the film or video image one step further by placing the individual 'inside' alternative worlds. By directly tinkering with reality, a simulation practice is set in place which alters forever the conditions under which the identity of the self is formed.
>
> (1995, p. 30–1)

Poster importantly makes the claim that virtual worlds and their simulations will alter 'the conditions under which the identity of the self is formed.' Further, he also states virtual worlds are different from real reality in that they evoke play and discovery. From Poster's observations and theories comes a suggestion that the play and discovery experienced in virtual or alternate realities might have some bearing on an individual's concept of the self, and therefore on the development of sexual ethics. The ethics of real reality may have little bearing on the ethics of alternate realities. This creates important considerations for how the simulation of ethical codes may tinker with the construction of ethical selves.

Much like Foucault's observed shift in ethical codes concerning marriage in the move from classical to imperial eras, Poster's postulations about a shift in methods of communication from modern to postmodern eras argue there is an effect on the self through a shift in relations to others. In both, a shift in communication and relationality influences an individual's subject constitution. For Foucault, the universal enforcement of the laws of marriage changed the ways in which men conceptualised themselves and their relationships to others to form a 'new stylistics of existence.' Likewise, the duplication and simulation of virtuality, for Poster, alters the conditions that form the 'identity of the self.' From a combination of theories on ethical subject constitution and new media comes an idea that erotic role-play, as a type of new sexual ethics based in the virtual, can allow for an alternate subjectivisation and conceptualisation of the sexual self. This is done not only through a reduction in the burden of real-life discourse and rules but also through an increased role of the imagination invoked when entering simulational, virtual worlds. Through research, this book attempts to assess the validity of this claim and whether or not erotic role-play, through its abstraction from reality and the power and knowledge present there, creates new ways for the constitution of ethical sexual selves.

PROBLEMATIC SEXUAL CONTENT IN GAMES

As previously discussed, the relationship between sex and games is full of tension. This is partially due to the already highlighted cultural prejudice that suggests games and playful activities are intended for children and not adults. When a behaviour normally coded as adult, such as sex or violence, becomes available for play, problems arise. These problems often take the form of public outcry, media panic, or legal response. In order to further our understanding of the relationship that games and sexuality share, it is important to consider examples in which sexual content in games has been identified as problematic.

For the most part, games have been criticised for their reluctance to engage with sexuality overall (Krzywinska 2012; Gallagher 2012). Although there are, of course, examples of games that have infolded sex into the plot to great effect – the *Dragon Age* series (BioWare 2009; 2011) taken as one such example – these games tend to be the exception rather than the rule. More common is for sex to be excluded from games, glossed over, or treated as a punchline. Mia Consalvo (2003), for example, points out the majority of romances represented in games follows a highly traditional fairytale model, in that heterosexual monogamy is the default, unexamined choice afforded to players. Taken as an example of the punchline approach, the infamous Hot Coffee Mod for the already controversial *Grand Theft Auto: San Andreas* (Rockstar Games 2004) was leaked in 2005. The Hot Coffee mod allowed players to access a hidden mini game in which the main-character, Carl CJ Johnson, has sex with his chosen in-game girlfriend. The minigame, which was hidden in the game's original coding and discovered by players of the personal-computer version of the game, caused controversy within industry review boards. Public pressure in North America led the Entertainment Software Review Board (ESRB) to change the game's classification from Mature (M) to Adults Only 18+ (AO). Interestingly, the Pan European Game Information system (PEGI) had already given *Grand Theft Auto: San Andreas* an 18+ rating and so the discovery of the Hot Coffee mod did not affect how the game was sold.

The Hot Coffee mod example is useful in beginning discussions of the relationship digital games have to representations of sex, as it touches on several topical controversies and themes as well as notes a critical time period in which the classification and rating of games became important. The early two thousands saw an increase in activity from rating and review boards, particularly as they responded to the presence of sex in digital games. PEGI was founded in 2003, for example, and the ESRB changed its 'mature sexual themes' rating to 'sexual themes' in 2004. This unexplained change in wording from the ESRB, perhaps unintentionally, serves to highlight the expectation that games will either avoid the inclusion of sexual content or include it in a slapstick, immature way.

The inclusion of immature sexual references seems ironically to sit more easily with review boards. The PC, PlayStation 3, and Xbox 360 game *Saints Row: The Third* (Volition 2011) is a perfect example of this irony. During the Return to Steelport mission, the protagonist rescues an auto-tuned pimp from a BDSM club called The Safeword. The highlight of the mission is an action-film-styled chase in which the protagonist rides a chariot pulled by the auto-tuned pimp, Zimos, wearing nothing more than strips of leather. Several chariots, also pulled by men wearing studded leather harnesses, often referred to as 'gimp' suits, give chase and a shoot-out quick-time event closes the mission. The over-the-top style of the club, which includes glory-holes and dildo machines, the outfits of characters, and the dramatic action sequence, causes the Return to Steelport mission to have a light-hearted, comedic feel rather than erotic. Perhaps it is for this reason the game, despite explicit sexual content, avoided an Adults Only rating and received instead a Mature rating from the ESRB.

On the surface, the difference between an AO and M rating may seem trivial, in that there is little semantic difference between what qualifies as mature and what qualifies as suitable for eighteen-year-olds and older. The economic reality, however, is the rating of games determines the market they can be advertised to and which shops may sell the games. Due to individual company policy, chain retail outlets such as Walmart refuse to stock AO-rated titles. Losing out on Walmart as a potential retailer is a 'kiss of death' for most titles, as Polygon writer Ben Kuchera (2014) points out. Further, a list of AO rated games on the ESRB website demonstrates that out of thirty titles, twenty-seven have 'strong sexual content' or 'nudity' descriptors. The three games given the AO title for something other than sexual content include a social-media app named Power Chat for BlackBerry (Jumbuck Entertainment 2010), which has 'suggestive themes', Peak Entertainment Casinos (Peak Entertainment 1997), which has 'gambling', and Thrill Kill (Virgin Interactive 1998), which would have had 'animated blood and gore, animated violence' with sadomasochistic and sexual themes but it was never released (ESRB 2014)[2].

The ESRB's influence likewise extends into massive multiplayer online role-playing games (MMORPGs), even if unpredictable user interactions cannot be rated. One of the games this book focuses on, *World of Warcraft*, needed to involve game masters in monitoring player behaviour after its Teen ESRB rating was called into question in 2007. Fuelled by forum-based rumours of guilds engaging in 'extreme age-play', the development company responsible for the game, Blizzard Entertainment, intervened and disbanded one particular guild suspected of paedophilia to keep the game teen-friendly (Wachowski 2007). A few years later, continual complaints about erotic role-play at a specific location in the game caused Blizzard to officially patrol the area with the intent of punishing those engaging in the activity (Westbrook 2010). The moral panic that afflicted arcades decades earlier (Williams 2006) resurfaced as the popularity of MMORPGs grew and players and parents alike became confronted with the uncomfortable fact adults and children were playing together online.

Aside from controversies over the age of players engaging with sexual content and the role of rating review boards in dictating consumer choice, other research has highlighted the tendency of role-players to engage with sex problematically. In the foundational text *Shared Fantasy: Role-Playing Games as Social Worlds*, Gary Alan Fine (1983) noted the 'aggressive orientation' of his participants. In particular, he noted this aggression occasionally took the form of sexual violence, noting in particular that "frequently male nonplayer characters who have not hurt the party are executed and female nonplayer characters raped for sport" (p.44). Fine never mentions whether or not sex was ever used in a consensual or romantic format. Instead it is only discussed as being used for violence or misogyny. Similarly focusing on sexual violence in a multiuser dungeon (MUD) is the journalistic 'A Rape in Cyberspace' (Dibbell 1993). Like Fine's account of tabletop role-playing, Julian Dibbell's account focuses only on sexual violence and is one of few available narratives of what MUDs were like. From these early accounts it is difficult to tell if sexual performances and representations in role-playing communities were full of violence and hate or if the researchers encountered other types of sexual play but, for one reason or another, did not include it in their analysis.

The first time a rounded depiction of sexuality in virtual worlds emerged was in Sherry Turkle's (1995) book *Life on the Screen: Identity in the Age of the Internet*. Gender-swapping, fake-lesbian syndrome, infidelity, and play with identity are all discussed as aspects of the online experience within multiuser dungeons. More than just controlling an avatar or typing commands for that avatar to execute, virtual sex in Turkle's account involves the development of emotional reactions for a character. Although Turkle terms the activity virtual sex, her account of the act draws many parallels to erotic role-play in its structure, player-affordances, and outcome. She notes, "In cyberspace, this activity is not only common but, for many people, it is the centrepiece of their online experience" (1995, p. 223). Turkle's work importantly illustrates that not only was consensual sexual activity taking place in at least some MUDs but also it was an extremely important part of the experience of being virtual.

Along similar lines, early studies of MMORPGs also hinted sexual themes were present during role-play. Amongst discussions of the relationships between players and characters are suggestions of romantic connections. In her 2006 book *Play Between Worlds*, T.L. Taylor uses social-network analysis to demonstrate the sometimes romantic relationships between guildmates and their characters. Taylor's work further served to illustrate the often problematic connections between sex and gender politics present in games. Similar to the sexist player behaviours Fine observed around gaming tables, the sexualised design of female avatars functions to exclude some women or make them feel uncomfortable. In her research into *EverQuest* (*EQ*), Taylor noted, "women in EQ often struggle with the conflicting meanings around their avatars. … When faced with the character-creation screen, it can feel as if one is choosing the best of the worst" (2006, p. 110).

Like Taylor's experience in *EverQuest*, studies focusing on *World of Warcraft* have likewise noted the prevalence of 'kombat lingerie' and avatar customisation limitations. In her analysis of *World of Warcraft* as a potential playground for feminism, however, Hilde Corneliussen (2008) notes players have a greater choice in both the body shape of their avatars and how they are dressed. She notes several items in the game, such as tabards or undershirts, can be placed under or over armour for a more conservative look (2008). The issue of avatar representation is more than just a stylistic fashion choice, however, and Esther MacCallum-Stewart and Justin Parsler have noted that despite a greater choice in coverings, armour in *World of Warcraft* is still heavily sexualised for female avatars and not so for males. MacCallum-Stewart and Parsler note, "It is common to find that a piece of clothing that fully covers the male figure is overly revealing on a woman" (2008, p. 231). They go on to give the example of the infamous Black Mage-weave armour set, which on a male avatar appears as an unremarkable shirt and trousers but appears as stockings, suspenders, and a basque top on female avatars (MacCallum-Stewart and Parsler 2008).

Some literature on live action role-play (LARP) has looked at how game design influences players' experience of sexuality. Past research by Marcus Montola (2010) into a Nordic LARP entitled Gang Rape explores how players of the game willingly took on the uncomfortable roles of victims and rapists to experience the extreme emotions involved in a sexually violent act. Rather than deal with intimate or erotic feelings, however, Gang Rape was designed as a form of political protest to highlight the difficulty in convicting rapists in Sweden (Montola 2010). Although Montola's descriptions of players' reactions to the game does much to highlight the oscillation of frames utilised during play and how some game design elements actually force players out of the diegetic frame through deliberately flimsy character development, the purpose of extreme LARP games such as Gang Rape has less to do with erotic role-play and more to do with experimental psychology.

The current body of knowledge on erotic role-play has done much to point out key issues arising from the activity. Gender politics, the prevalence and controversy surrounding play with sexual violence, concern over adult content being made available for children, and the one-sided sexualisation of female avatars are all important issues surrounding the themes of sexuality and games. What is missing from this literature, however, is an account of how players engage with and make meaning out of sexual and erotic experiences during role-play. Role-play is a particularly interesting example, as we have seen in this chapter, because it makes obvious the multiple frames players experience at any given time. Further investigation is therefore needed into not only how players make sense of the activity but also who erotic role-players are.

NOTES

1. The earliest mention of which is found in *Jet Magazine*, 6 August 1953.
2. The search that led to these results was conducted on 2 September 2014 on the ESRB's website: http://www.esrb.org/ratings/search.jsp. It should be noted there were 40 titles which received the AO rating but 10 inexplicably did not include a descriptor/justification for the rating.

3   Erotic Role-Players

In 2005 T.L. Taylor invited readers of her book *Play Between Worlds* to think for a moment about gamers and the images such a term calls to mind. It is worth repeating this exercise here. Think for a moment about the term 'erotic role-player' and think about the images it conjures. What do erotic role-players look like? Who are they? What are their lives like? When Taylor asked her readers to do this activity, she was looking for the presumption to emerge that the average gamer is a young male. To some extent, this presumption applies to erotic role-players as well.

Erotic role-players occupy a unique intersection of gaming and sexuality that causes them to be associated with masculine gender characteristics. There are several reasons for this, which predominantly rely on the gendered signifiers of key aspects of the hobby, namely in its relation to games, sex, and the erotic. Given the residual stigma and taboo centred on women's expression of sexual pleasure[1] and the problematic assumption that libidinal urges are gender-specific, the idea that the majority of erotic role-players would be male emerges. Likewise, as Taylor's exercise points out, the image of the average videogame player, despite substantial evidence to the contrary (Entertainment Software Association 2013), is still a young man. Not just any young man, however, but a young man belonging to a particular social group with a particularly low social status. As evidenced by research on gamers' social positioning (Kowert, Griffiths, and Oldmeadow 2013), as well as images and caricatures in popular culture, those who play games are often typified as lacking social skills or otherwise socially awkward. The combination of these assumptions might lead to the image of erotic role-players as a particular type of young man who lacks the socialisation, or perhaps the desire, to be sexually active. The image that might emerge of erotic role-players' motivation to engage in the activity is that they turn to technology and games to remediate the kinds of pleasures that are not afforded them in other aspects of their lives. In order to dismantle this stereotype of erotic role-players, it is important first to consider what information is available about why people erotic role-play, who erotic role-plays, and how we gain this information.

Gaining information about erotic role-players is more difficult than it might seem, as they are a particularly difficult population to reach. Not only are topics relating to sex often uncomfortable to talk about, which surely may dissuade some erotic role-players from potentially participating in an academic study, but typically the practice is banned. Many online role-playing games disallow the use of specific sexual language in public chats so the game can achieve a lower parental-guidance rating and actively punish players breaking this rule with temporary or permanent account bans[2]. Likewise, for tabletop roleplayers many games take place in public settings, such as game shops, in which children may be present. The likelihood of encountering players outwardly engaging in erotic role-play in these settings is rare, and even if it were common, cold-calling such players for an interview would likely be an uncomfortable process for both participant and researcher. For players to even admit they engage in erotic role-play is for them to face a possible ban from the site of play, a loss of their gaming account, or derision and mockery from fellow players. For these reasons, careful consideration of sampling strategy as well as ethics is necessary to gain population access. Later in this chapter, after considering the motivations and demographics of players, time will be spent discussing the methodology of the research that informed this book and the unique challenges encountered when gathering participants for this study.

PLAYER MOTIVATIONS

One of the first questions we might ask in order to understand who erotic role-plays is what motivations there might be for engaging in the activity. Like all forms of role-playing, the practice is extraordinarily resource-consuming. Players spend countless hours reading expensive rulebooks, looking up lore, printing inspirational material, drawing characters, communicating with other players, thinking about their character's personality and interests, planning campaigns, and countless other activities that contribute to the hobby overall. This is as true of tabletop erotic role-play as it is of online variations. Aside from the claim it is fun, which is an important claim but one that achieves an analytical dead end as many other games and hobbies that are less resource-consuming are likely also fun, it is worth exploring what past research has found about what motivates players to undertake such an activity. Unfortunately, no past research addresses the motivations for erotic role-play directly. There is, however, plenty of research that addresses the motivations of role-players more generally. This is a useful starting point for discussions of motivations because, as we shall see in subsequent chapters, participants often view erotic role-play as enfolding erotic content into existing role-play scenarios and not as a separate hobby altogether. The description of player motivations will begin with tabletop role-playing and then discuss online variations.

Tabletop role-playing games can generally be defined as a genre of games that requires players to temporarily take on the identity of a fictional character and play the role of that character in an imaginary world. An academic definition of role-playing games defines them as "any game which allows a number of players to assume the roles of imaginary characters and operate with some degree of freedom in an imaginary environment" (Lortz 1979, p. 36). The use of the term 'tabletop' as a prefix to 'role-playing games' references a specific type of RPG that is most commonly played around a table. Players use rulebooks, pieces of paper, pencils, and dice to play such games. Past research has additionally pointed out this type of role-playing "is oral, and does not involve physical acting" and "the players or the referee [dungeon or game master] must roll dice to determine the outcome of battles or other encounters among players" (Fine 1983, p. 7). The use of dice is important as they "determine (through the rules) who is killed or the extent of the injury, or provide some formal structure for an otherwise *very* flexible game" (Fine 1983, p. 7, emphasis original). The ludic mechanic of rolling dice, in conjunction with rules that dictate how the dice are rolled, importantly differentiate tabletop role-playing from other types of play. The rules that govern how tabletop games are played are sold in the form of handbooks and player guides in hobbyist shops and bookstores alike. As this description hopefully makes clear, to engage in tabletop role-play is to invest time and other resources into playing a narrative-driven game with flexible rules that heavily relies on the imagination, storytelling, and creative abilities of players and game master.

Past research on the motivations of tabletop role-playing is limited, with only one ethnographic study by Gary Alan Fine (1983) that specifically deals with the topic. Fine has found tabletop role-players can be characterised as 'nonconformists' (Fine 1983). Support for this characterisation comes from the previously detailed intense time and monetary commitment the activity requires. In addition to purchasing dice, rulebooks, and other materials required for the gaming to take place, immense amounts of time are required to not only play the game but also for players to make themselves familiar with the rules and settings before play can begin. In his ethnography on fantasy role-players, Gary Alan Fine writes this intense commitment "precludes participation in other activities that are considered 'normal' ('social life', stylish clothing, or knowledge of television shows)" (1983, p. 45). Through interviews, Fine's research points out players distinguish themselves from 'the average Joe on the street' and feel their role-playing hobby differentiates them from 'normal' or 'average' people (1983, p. 46). In summarising participant responses about how tabletop role-players differentiate themselves from 'the average Joe', Fine writes, "Joe' is a man with so many normative commitments that he has no time, energy or inclination for active fantasy. His fantasy is passive, deriving from television violence, sports, and the undulations of the sex goddesses of prime-time entertainment" (1983, p. 46). The way in which players in Fine's study differentiated themselves from the average Joe who watches the 'undulations of the sex goddesses of prime-time entertainment' points out that while both groups may find entertainment and recreation through titillation, the tabletop role-players view themselves as taking an active role in the creation of sexualised entertainment, and perhaps create and experience sexuality through it. In the self-defined division of Fine's participants from larger society and the resulting cultural experiences comes a notion that role-players exist on the fringes of mainstream popular culture.

Considering the large investment of time and resources required by tabletop role-playing, it is important to consider the justifications players give for engaging in the activity and what draws people to an activity that demands such active investment. As might be expected of research into recreation and play, and as mentioned above, the primary justification given for tabletop role-playing is that it is fun. Efforts have been made, however, to go beyond fun and look at additional justifications given for the hobby. Fine breaks down the explanations given by his participants into four themes: educational gains, escapism, personal control or efficacy, and aids for social interaction (1983, p. 53). Each of these themes will be discussed below.

Following from the earlier assertion that tabletop RPGs require a large time investment, Fine found players often viewed the background reading necessary to participate in games as a type of educational endeavour. He notes that whilse "these games do not provide realistic depictions of ... medieval Europe," serious discussions about the practicalities of "such things as the weight of plate armour, the social structure of the Catholic Church in twelfth-century France" do occur (1983, p. 54). In addition to such discussions, tabletop RPGs were additionally viewed by informants in his study as increasing aptitude in a number of real-life behavioural skills such as information synthesis, decision-making, leadership, and role-playing as a type of acting (Fine 1983). From this research comes the idea that participants view role-playing as a type of learning experience. Be it information or skills, the emergence of education as an explanation for play points out that at least some role-players view the activity as having the potential to transfer knowledge and skills from in-game to real life. This may have interesting implications for erotic role-play and whether or not the skills and knowledges gained from engaging with erotic content in play can also transfer into real life.

The second explanation given in Fine's research is escapism. He defines this as an "escape from the constraints of the players' mundane reality" (1983, p. 54). Players in his study discussed RPGs as an escape from two related components: constructions of the self and restrictions on behaviour. Relying on field notes, Fine discusses his initial shock at how rarely players discussed their personal lives within tabletop groups and gives the example of how only after months of playing within such a group did he learn players' surnames. In a combination of observations and interviews, Fine attributes his and other players' experiences as a form of escaping their real self. He attributes the lack of exchanged personal information as a result of role-playing. In undertaking a character or persona for the duration of a game, emphasis is placed on playing the role of a fictional character instead of portraying one's true self (Fine 1983). This distancing of the self plays a role in the second observed form of escapism.

Fine uses the example of the often aggressive and violent behaviour of characters within RPGs and participants' justification of that behaviour as a 'psychological blow valve' indicative of an escape from the constraints of everyday life. He writes, "While such [violent] activities are a legitimate part of the game, they also require legitimation since they provide *prima facie* evidence of players' immorality. The rhetoric of escape with its justification that such behaviour prevents aggression preserves the moral integrity of players" (Fine 1983, p. 57). From Fine's research comes the idea that tabletop role-playing provides an escape from players' mundane lives and an escape from social behavioural constraints. From this assessment, tabletop RPGs can be thought of as providing an escape from formulations of morality and considerations of the self as subject to ethical constraints. Merging the findings of this research with the previous chapter's use of Foucault, a view of tabletop role-playing emerges that can be said to foster an escape from the self and from normative ethical expectations, which could potentially allow for experimentation with non-normative sexuality. This book aims to assess if this is possible.

The third justification present in Fine's research is that tabletop RPGs give players a sense of control and efficacy. This theme is connected to the previous one of escapism through informants' juxtaposition of their mundane lives as being out of their control alongside the lives of their characters, which they can control. Although characters are in many ways subjected to the rules of a game, actions of other players, and ultimately the game master, Fine discovered some tabletop role-players viewed role-playing as a "testing of boundaries, [which enabled] players to learn about themselves in situations of controlled danger" (1983, p. 58). In this sense, 'controlled danger' makes reference to the limited transferability of consequences for actions between the game world and the real world. In addition to this idea of limited transferability, role-playing was seen as efficacious through its ability to allow self-authorship. Rather than watching a film or reading a book, players felt they were actively engaged with creating a story when playing an RPG. The efficacy involved in creating an original story combined with controlled danger has potential implications for erotic role-play. From Fine's past research comes a suggestion that players may justify their erotic role-play by citing tabletop RPG's affordance for character and environmental control, as well as the ability to manage danger in games. Sexuality's perceived threats to the moral and physical health of players may be viewed as manageable or controllable, and thus players might feel they have the efficacy to experiment with non-normative sexual behaviours.

The final justification present in Fine's research is that of social interaction. Fine (1983) compares the results of his interviews with tabletop role-players as similar to social bonding in other types of hobbies and activities, but he carefully points out that due to role-players' self-identification as being different from the average Joe, social interaction in other circumstances may be strained. Indeed, past research into tabletop role-playing groups has shown players often have difficulty interacting with others, particularly women, outside of game contexts (Holmes 1981). Fine's own participants reported tabletop role-playing facilitated the acquisition and use of social skills either by bonding over a common hobby or through interacting to reach goals (1983). By justifying tabletop role-play through positive social interaction and the acquisition of social skills, past research seems to suggest two important themes for consideration. The first is that tabletop role-players may be less adept at social interaction than their non-role-playing counterparts, and the second is that they may use tabletop role-playing for socialisation, particularly in groups within which they might not otherwise interact.

Now that literature on the motivations of tabletop role-players has been reviewed, attention needs to be given to massive multiplayer online role-playing games (MMORPGs). MMORPGs can be simply defined as digital role-playing games that use the Internet to allow for interactivity between hundreds or even thousands of players simultaneously. Like the RPGs discussed in the previous section, definitions for this genre place emphasis on playing the role, or temporarily taking on the identity, of an imaginary character in an imaginary world. Unlike tabletop RPGs, however, MMORPGs use computers to provide players with graphic representations of characters and the world the characters inhabit.

A more nuanced definition of the genre was developed by Andrew Burn and Diane Carr during their study of *Anarchy Online*. They describe it as, first, a role-playing game "in that players construct and develop their protagonist, join teams (if they choose) and 'level up' in specialist skills" (2006, p. 26), but note it is different from other RPGs in that it is online. The online component of MMORPGs "means that players collectively inhabit and shape the events of a persistent, shared game world" (Burn and Carr 2006, p. 26). Unlike digital role-playing games without Internet access, when the player logs out of an MMORPG, the virtual world persists and events, quests, and activities keep occurring. In addition to this broad definition, a more succinct definition of role-playing in MMORPGs defines the act as "limiting one's talk to entities and events of the fictitious game world and avoiding references to the physical world or their offline identities" (Williams, Kennedy, and Moore 2010, p. 173). So in addition to playing within a persistent online world with many other users, role-players within these worlds embrace a style of playing similar to tabletop role-playing.

Just as Gary Alan Fine noted RPGs appealed to participants because they offered "an escape from players' mundane reality" (1983, p. 54), Sherry Turkle's (1995) past research on multi-user dungeons (MUDs) found role-players were an especially troubled group and chose to role-play as a form of escape during an especially trying time in their lives. Likewise, quantitative studies on the reasons players give for playing MMORPGs, including *World of Warcraft*, have found many players also cite escapism as a primary motivation to play (Yee 2006; Caplana, Williams and Yee 2009; Williams, Kennedy, and Moore 2010). Such studies on MMORPGs have attempted to problematise escapism, choosing to read its use as a justification for playing as indicative of players' inability to cope with the stresses of everyday life (Kinney 1993; Yee 2006; Caplana, Williams, and Yee 2009). However, as Fine notes in his ethnography, all leisure pursuits permit "a sanctioned disengagement from the constraints of the 'serious' world" (1983, p. 54). Football players, golfers, and other non-fantasy and non-RPG hobbyists are rarely the subjects of inquiry into how their chosen method of disengagement reflects their psychological profile. For this reason, I contend that although the population of this study may use erotic role-play as a form of escapism from real-life stress, they need not necessarily be considered any more at risk of psychological or physical health problems than other groups of hobbyists. This is especially the case since no causal relationship has been established between role-play and health risks. Additionally, past research has noted role-play was positively viewed by participants as a 'relaxing break' rather than a total escape from the problems of reality (Williams, Kennedy, and Moore 2010).

In addition to escapism, previous research has found immersion to be a key motivation to role-play (Williams, Kennedy, and Moore 2010). Immersion is a popular concept in the field of game-studies literature and has been defined as a "metaphorical term derived from the physical experience of being submerged in water ... the sensation of being surrounded by a completely other reality, as different as water is from air, that takes over all of our attention, our whole perceptual apparatus" (Murray 1997, pp. 98-99). However, past research has read into immersion as more than just a shift in perception. Relying on interview data, Williams, Kennedy, and Moore (2010) found that for their participants, immersion was a form of identity experimentation. Similar to Fine's (1983) reading of escapism from social constraints, immersion for MMORPG role-players "revolved more around a person being able to express things they were socially constrained from doing off-line" (Williams, Kennedy, and Moore 2010, p. 188). The specific example Williams, Kennedy, and Moore give is flirting. They noted some players chose to role-play characters with flirty personalities and for these players, such personality experimentation bled over into their offline behaviours. This has important connotations for erotic role-play as it suggests character behaviours, such as flirting, may cross over from the game world into the daily lives and behaviours of participants.

Existing literature has not deeply explored the extent to which this crossover might occur for MMORPG players, although some investigation has been done in regards to live-action role-play (LARP). Past research into LARPs has found strong emotional reactions to in-character events sometimes bleed into out-of-character feelings between participants (Bowman 2011; Montola 2010). Because past research has found immersion, escapism, and a desire to express otherwise constrained behaviours as motivations and justifications for role-play, and there has been some past research that hints there is potential for the behaviours to bleed into players' real lives, Chapter Six addresses whether the behaviours expressed in ERP cross over.

Past research suggests role-players play to temporarily escape real-life issues and problems and to experiment with different behaviours and personalities. Although this information is useful in providing a description of who role-players are and why they role-play, past studies have failed to consider to what extent crossover occurs. Whilst past studies found role-play had the potential to bleed into real life, either through behaviours, emotions, or the transfer of communication skills, there is a distinct lack of discussion on how this might refer to sexuality. The absence of such discussion seems particularly amiss considering past research has discovered role-players disproportionately come from sexual-minority backgrounds. The motivations of erotic role-players, as well as what effects this might have on their lives outside the game, will be discussed in Chapter Six. From this general overview of the motivations of role-players, the next section will specifically discuss what is currently known about the demographics of role-players.

PLAYER DEMOGRAPHICS

Because of the difficulty in studying this particular population, there is no existing demographical information specifically about erotic role-players. As mentioned before, no database exists that contains information about who erotic role-players are. There are, however, a few studies that have been able to gain some insight into the demographics of role-players. For online digital games this is a much easier and much more accurate task to complete than it is for those interested in tabletop populations. Nevertheless, going through existing statistics will give better insight into who role-plays, and as erotic role-play is a type of role-play, this will provide some information about who might erotic role-play on a larger scale than is represented in this book. After a general overview of existing statistics, demographic information specific to the participants in this study will be given to situate the population that informed this research within a larger context. Although, given the sampling methods employed to collect data for this book, it is not possible to generalise to a larger population, it is helpful to demonstrate the erotic role-play participants of this study match the known demographic information found in past research.

Existing research into the demographics of tabletop role-players is rare. A 1979 survey of readers of the popular tabletop magazine *The Dragon*[3], published by Tactical Studies Rules Incorporated, the same publishers of the popular tabletop game *Dungeons and Dragons* (*D&D*), revealed the median age of their readership was between 22 and 30 years old (cited in Fine 1983, p. 40). In Gary Alan Fine's personal communication with Gary Gygax, the writer and developer of *Dungeons and Dragons*, Gygax estimated that between ten to fifteen percent of all *D&D* players are women (1983, p. 41). Tabletop RPGs appear to be a male-dominated activity (Fine 1983), which has significant implications for how sexuality and erotic content may enter into the games.

Although the estimated numbers provided by Gygax and *The Dragon* have likely changed over time as tabletop role-playing has gained popularity, there are few reliable ways of measuring the age and gender of tabletop role-players. Many methods used in the past with some success, such as monitoring role-playing convention attendance, are impossible now. With attendees of such events reaching the thousands, simple door polls become difficult. Likewise, with regards to maintaining attendee privacy or perhaps in the interest of conserving valuable marketing data, convention organisers are reluctant to divulge demographic data to researchers. Even if accessing such data were possible, the data would only be representative of role-playing convention-goers and not actual role-players. Presumably there are many role-players who would like to attend such conventions but for one reason or another choose not to, and they would be excluded from such a study. Conversely, there are likely to be many attendees of role-playing conventions who do not role-play themselves but are there because they are drawn to other aspects of convention-going.

The tabletop group that informed this study consisted of only three players other than myself. The reasons for this number, as well as how they were recruited, will be detailed in the methods section below. For now it is worth noting all three participants more or less match Fine's (1983) description of tabletop role-players. The three players were all based in the northwest of England, where they had grown up. The youngest participant was 22 years old and the oldest 26 at the time of the interview. Two self-identify as gay men and one identifies as a bisexual man.

Collecting demographic data about players of MMORPGs, on the other hand, is much less challenging. In order to play an MMORPG, potential users must purchase the game, register an account, and pay a monthly fee[4]. Part of the registration process usually requires users to submit personal information about their age, gender, and play habits. Because of this, and the relatively easy accessibility of players through online communication[5], rich demographic information about who plays MMORPGs is available. In a large study of 6,675 players spanning over three years and multiple MMORPGs, Nick Yee found eighty-five percent of players were male and the average age of respondents was 26.5 years (2006). Yee's research helps to debunk the commonly held assumption that MMORPG players are teenagers and students by further finding that half of respondents worked full time (2006). Whilst these figures give some indication as to who plays

MMORPGs, Yee's research relied on a convenience sample of players and additionally did not take into consideration individual players' preferences for play style. Not all in Yee's sample were in fact role-players.

A richer demographical account for role-players, as a subset of MMORPG players, is given in the work of Dmitri Williams, Tracey Kennedy, and Robert Moore (2010). In an unprecedented case, Williams, Kennedy, and Moore worked with Sony Entertainment to not only analyse demographic records kept by the company but also to use stratified sampling to survey specific groups of players of *Everquest II*. From their research, it was found dedicated role-players, those that preferred to remain in-character at all times, represented only five percent of MMORPG players overall (Williams, Kennedy, and Moore 2010, p. 108). Additionally, they found that compared to infrequent role-players, dedicated role-players tended to be slightly younger (28.55 years compared to 30.55 years), have more women players (twenty-five percent), be slightly less educated, and be from a sexual, religious, or racial minority (2010, p. 183). The study additionally found a direct correlation between the amount of time spent role-playing and the likelihood of a player having been clinically diagnosed with physical or mental problems (Williams, Kennedy, and Moore 2010, p. 108).

From past research, the demographic information about role-players seems to suggest they are mostly male, in their late twenties, from minority groups, and have impediments to physical and mental health. Additionally, past research suggests only a small percentage of players in MMORPGs role-play, thus forming a type of minority group within groups of players overall. Such a characterisation of players not only resonates with previous descriptions of tabletop role-players but additionally provides insight into why they might be drawn to role-play. As detailed in the above section on motivations for play, some role-players reported using the activity as a type of 'psychological blow valve' (Fine 1983, p. 57) and a form of escapism during times of difficulty (Turkle 1995).

The participants of this study in some ways fit the previous demographical descriptions of MMORPG players but were quite different in others. In total, fourteen guild members of varying ages, genders, and sexual preferences volunteered to be interviewed during the nine months of fieldwork. There were seven women participants, six men participants, and one transgendered participant. Their ages ranged from twenty to forty-one years old with a mean age of twenty-nine. The age of the participants is similar to the average age (28.55 years) reported by the Williams, Kennedy, and Moore (2010) study; however the representation of gender is not. Additionally, although I did not specifically ask about sexual orientation, through the course of most interviews participants volunteered how they identified themselves within the spectrum of sexuality. This usually emerged either through a question about how their out-of-game sexual partner(s) viewed their in-game erotic play or through a question that asked them to explain the similarities and differences between themselves and their character. In total, five participants identified as bisexual, six as heterosexual, one as lesbian, and two as unsure/questioning. There is no current demographic information to compare this to.

THE METHODOLOGY OF GETTING TO KNOW
EROTIC ROLE-PLAYERS

In order to answer the primary research question – whether erotic role-play in tabletop and MMORPG communities provides alternate ways to express sexuality – a methodology needed to be adopted that would account for both the nature and location of interaction in tabletop and *World of Warcraft* erotic role-play. Likewise, research methods were needed that would take into consideration the interpretive work required on the part of the researcher to situate the phenomenon of erotic role-play within a larger understanding of social worlds. This is particularly the case when considering what is currently known about erotic role-players: they are a small group of less than five percent of all MMORPG players and are particularly open to misrepresentation. In order to minimise the likelihood of misrepresentation, an epistemology that considers experience a type of data was adopted.

To embrace the ideas included in such an epistemology, I adopted an interpretivist, qualitative, ethnographic framework for the collection and interpretation of data. This allows for my experiential knowledge of the community and the phenomenon of erotic role-play to be included in the research in a meaningful way. As Kathy Charmaz writes, "We can know a world by describing it from the outside. Yet to understand what living in this world means, we need to learn from the inside. Starting from the inside is the initial step to developing a rich qualitative analysis" (2004, p. 980). This potentially rich qualitative analysis arising from insider research brings with it with problems of bias, as detailed above, and also raises ethical problems that will be considered at the end of this chapter. For now, however, the focus will be on my decision to use ethnographic, qualitative methods.

After considering my insider position as someone who role-plays and has encountered erotic role-play in the field prior to research, I decided the best framework to gain further knowledge and insight into how this community plays with concepts like sexuality would be to conduct an ethnography centred on experiencing erotic role-play as it occurs organically in imaginary worlds. Christine Hine provides a concise and easily accessible definition of ethnography as "a way of seeing through participants' eyes: a grounded approach that aims for a deep understanding of the cultural foundations of the group" (2000, p. 21). Importantly for the fieldwork, "contemporary ethnography thus belongs to a tradition of 'naturalism' which centralises the importance of understanding meanings and cultural practices of people from within the everyday settings in which they take place" (O'Connell, Davidson, and Layder 1994, p. 165). Perhaps for these reasons of embeddedness, ethnographies have been used as tools to study both tabletop role-playing groups (Fine 1983) and online role-playing communities in the past (Taylor 2006; Turkle 1995). In previous research into online gaming communities, ethnographies have been favoured because they "do not claim to generate factual truths that can be generalised from a sample group onto the population as a whole, as in quantitative, survey-based sociology" (Kirkpatrick 2009, p. 21). This is an important facet of the research, as the aim is not to generalise findings for gamers as a whole but rather to describe the actions of players partaking in a particular type of role-playing. In terms of the individual methods undertaken, I conducted a textual analysis of rulebooks, individual interviews and focus groups with players, participant observation, and case studies. Each of these will be described in turn.

TEXTUAL ANALYSIS

In order to understand the sexual discourses and rules present in erotic role-play, I conducted a textual analysis. The texts for analysis were directly referred to in the interview and focus-group data and were analysed according to an interpretivist approach. By interpretivist approach I mean one which is "concerned with understanding the social world people have produced and which they reproduce through their continuing activities" (Blaikie 2000, p. 15). The books included in this interpretivist analysis are *Werewolf: The Apocalypse* (Rein-Hagen et al. 1994), *Vampire: The Masquerade* (Rein-Hagen 1992), *Vampire: The Requiem* (Marmell et al. 2004), *The Book of Vile Darkness* (Cook et al. 2002), *World of Warcraft: Horde Player's Guide* (Johnson 2006), *Book of the Wyrm* (Campbell et al. 1998), and *Freak Legion: A Player's Guide to the Fomori* (Bridges 1995). Rather than read each of these books cover to cover, only relevant, participant-referenced sections were read for assistance in interpreting interview and focus-group data. As has been mentioned in previous research within role-play communities (Fine 1983), participants had such a thorough familiarity with the text that they were able to specify references to rules and abilities nearly to the page number.

Overall, the research uses interpretive analysis of rulebooks to specifically look at rules and themes relating to sexuality within games and how they are used by erotic role-players. These rules and themes are considered a type of discourse that influences players' treatment of erotic themes and erotic role-play, but this discourse is not read inflexibly as is typical of discourse analysis. It is read within the participants' "everyday reality [that] consists of the meanings and interpretations given by the social actors to their actions, other people's actions, social situations, and natural and humanly created objects" (Blaikie 2000, p. 115). So although the rules themselves are considered a type of discourse, they are read and analysed within the experiences and interpretations of both participants and researcher.

ENTERING THE FIELD AND PARTICIPANT RECRUITMENT

The tabletop role-playing group and *World of Warcraft* guild of which I was already a member were chosen as the 'locations' or group settings for study. In addition to previous statements made about the importance of grounding interpretative research in the experiences of participants and researcher (Charmaz 2004; Hine 2000), these groups were chosen as sites for study due to my familiarity with the groups. Rather than view my existing familiarity with participants as problematic for the collection and interpretation of data, I view it as integral to my ontological and epistemological approach that considered participant experience of virtual social worlds as data. Although I was already a member of the communities, I still needed to enter the field officially as a researcher before observation could begin. This was accomplished in two ways. First, I needed to negotiate access and gain the consent of the gate-keepers and participants to be studied, and secondly I needed to inform and make clear to the groups that my role would shift from player to researcher.

The tabletop group consisted of only three players, aside from myself, and so securing access and consent involved an informal conversation before one of our routine role-play sessions. In this case, there was no formal gate-keeper to approach, not only because of the size of the group but also because all three of the participants more or less shared an equal role and equal participation in the role-playing that took place. Additionally, the three participants, Joe, Scott, and Dan,[6] were familiar both with me and each other. I had been role-playing with them for over a year at the time fieldwork began, and they had been role-playing as well as socialising together for at least two years. The familiarity between the participants is important to note because I interpret their interactions, especially during the focus group, as demonstrative of a pre-existing group dynamic. I feel this group dynamic influenced their responses to the focus-group questions. Below is an excerpt from my research notes detailing how they were recruited and their initial response to my offers of compensation for their participation.

24 October 2010
Talked to the primary dungeon masters/storytellers[7] about doing an interview and what they wanted in return for their time. They said nothing because they wanted to help and they have been "guinea pigs" for research before. I think this is symptomatic of the tabletop group being university educated. They have all known someone doing a dissertation. I think I will provide food and drinks for them during the interviews.

Much like the tabletop group, my familiarity with a few of the *World of Warcraft* guild members undoubtedly affected my approach to the research as well as the findings, which will be covered in greater depth shortly. The first step in entering the game as a researcher rather than as a player was to ask the guild leaders, as gate-keepers, for permission to study the guild they organise and run. This was not only a courteous gesture to the leaders but also a good way to reintroduce myself as a researcher to the players I already knew and to introduce myself to the players I had not yet met. In a guild of over 120 members with varying schedules and play times, it was difficult to meet everyone. In a guild setting, players trust guild leaders to give direction to the group's play by planning events, communicating with other guilds to meet goals, and taking care of problems, such as arguments, within the guild itself. As a result, many players place a significant amount of trust in their guild leaders, and once I had established an amiable relationship with them and explained my research, this trust was transferred to me.

To enter the field as a researcher and notify guild members that research was being conducted, I created an account on the guild's forums. I additionally created and maintained a profile with information about me, the research, and a link to my university-affiliated web page. The forum profile was useful in providing evidence I was who I professed to be and my research was genuine. Additionally, it provided contact information for members interested in participating in either the interview or observation process. I also created a post in the guild forum detailing important information about the research project and what it would entail. Through this post, I asked players interested in participating to send a private message through e-mail, the forum, or in the game. I also made it clear that due to privacy issues, I would never publically approach players and ask for their participation.

PARTICIPANT OBSERVATIONS

Because the ontological perspective of the research "sees interactions, actions and behaviours and the way people interpret these, act on them, and so on, as central" (Mason 2002, p. 85), participant observation was selected as a research method. As already discussed, the epistemological approach for the book additionally considers "that knowledge or evidence of the social world can be generated by observing or participating in, or experiencing, 'natural' or 'real-life' settings, interactive situations and so on" (Mason 2002, p. 85)[8]. Not only does participant observation allow for interview data to be situated within a deeper, complex account of how erotic role-play is done but it additionally allowed me to gain experience and insider knowledge of how the participants themselves view the activity. Participant observation allowed me to see how rules that banned erotic role-play, in the case of *World of Warcraft*, were negotiated by participants and how rules that guided erotic behaviour were implemented *de facto*. Additionally, participant observation provided a first-hand account of how communities of erotic role-players discussed and viewed the act.

Originally, the tabletop observations were set to take place three Sundays a month for one year around my kitchen table, but this proved impractical due to the daily lives of players and the relegation of play as a leisure activity. Although the group met most Sundays, occasionally a session would be cancelled due to holidays or late Saturday nights out. In addition to this, the group's role-playing campaigns would typically only last for six to eight sessions before the story came to a natural end or the group became bored with the content and moved on to a new story. The campaigns, or stories, take months of planning and writing to complete so there would often be additional down time while new stories and characters were being configured. Rather than view this as an inconvenience to the limited time I had available to spend in the field, I saw it as indicative of the players' dedication to role-playing.

During the tabletop participant observation, I had intended to take notes about topics relating to sexuality, gender, or erotic role-play as they emerged during play sessions. However, a few weeks into fieldwork I discovered my careful note-taking generated an overabundance of largely irrelevant data. Additionally, it was also difficult to perform the task of both player and researcher at the same time, with good note-taking coming at the expense of participating and good role-playing at the expense of good research. To compromise, the notes were taken in abbreviated ways. Often I would write a few key words to recall a particular event or scenario, which would then be recorded at length in a typed document the following day. These notes helped to provide examples of erotic play, background information about individual participants, and informed and contextualised subsequent analysis.

The *World of Warcraft* participant observation was primarily used to get a general feel for the game and the culture of role-playing and being in a guild. The emphasis was placed on participation and less on observation. In a marked difference to the tabletop group, I found I had little control over the environment in which the *World of Warcraft* research was conducted. Because *World of Warcraft* is a 'persistent world' (Burn and Carr 2006), in that players can log in and out of the game without a perceivable disruption to other players, there was no way I could only observe participants who had signed the informed consent and not other players who did not want to participate. For this reason, the various chat systems within the game (such as guild, raid, and general chats) were not monitored. I did not want to accidentally record non-participating guild members, nor did I want to disrupt the community's organic interactions through monitoring their chat.

Although I did not record chat logs of any in-game events, I did keep a research diary and noted I attended various events, such as guild meetings, a wedding, and a 'hen night', and how my participation in these events effected the development of my character and her relationships with other players. However, due to my previous promise to not monitor the guild's activities, these notes were written vaguely. Instead of specific details, such as character names or direct quotes, I focused on my own perception of what had occurred and the general feelings the experience left me with. This was done to help monitor impression management and my subjective feelings towards participants, which will be outlined in section three of this chapter. An example of my research-diary notes about the 'hen night' follows:

> 9 February 2011
> Stayed up late (2 AM) to attend a 'hen night' party involving members of the guild and their friends. I was shocked to see just how many characters showed up. In celebration, my character ended up getting drunk and joining in the bawdy humour and banter. I found myself smiling, laughing, and genuinely enjoying the event on an out-of-character level. Better than any 'real life' night out I've had in a long time.

During this phase of the research, I additionally was a regular and active member of the guild's forums. In my introductory letter, I had informed participants I would regularly read and check specific areas of the forums as part of the research. From these observations I developed questions in the interview guides that asked about participant-created artwork and fan fiction, and with the author's or artist's permission, used excerpts or examples of the work for analysis. Additionally, notes were taken, but never direct quotes, about how the forums were used. For example, it was noted members would often provide constructive criticism or comment on how they enjoyed posted erotic artwork.

FOCUS GROUP WITH TABLETOP PARTICIPANTS

In addition to the participant observation, a focus group was conducted with the tabletop participants. A focus group was chosen over individual interviews so I could observe "how situational interactions take place, and how issues are conceptualised, worked out, and negotiated in those contexts" (Mason 2002, p. 64). Because the tabletop group played with erotic themes in a physical, face-to-face setting together, I wanted the data to reflect how topics for play emerged from group decision-making. In a classic text, David Morgan claims "the hallmark of focus groups is the explicit use of the group interaction to produce data and insights that would be less accessible without the interaction found in a group" (1988, p. 12). Accordingly, it was useful to have the participants together so they could reflect on their erotic play and explain the nuances they had communally constructed.

Morgan also tells us "focus groups are useful when it comes to investigating what participants think, but they excel at uncovering why participants think as they do" (1988, p. 25). Morgan's quote becomes particularly useful when reading the transcripts from the focus group. Much of the banter I had observed and noted during the participant observations was clearly present during the focus group, which undoubtedly provided insight into not only how the group communicated but how they measured their words and actions from each other's reactions. Additionally, because the ontology of the research wanted to look at the creation or implementation of discourse and the effects on players' conceptualisations of sexual, ethical selves in game play, it made sense in this case to include the group dynamic of table-top role-playing in the research methodology. Past research into the ways in which people discuss their sexual selves has likewise found that:

> No longer do people simply 'tell' their sexual stories to reveal the 'truth' of their sexual lives; instead they turn themselves into socially organised biographical objects. They construct – even invent, though that may be too crass a term – tales of the intimate self, which may or may not bear a relationship to a truth.
>
> (Plummer 1995, p. 34)

This is particularly the case with erotic role-playing, since by its very nature it is a co-authored and communally told type of story. Plummer goes on to explain:

> The proliferation of sexual stories, then, is connected to a proliferation of sexual consumption – stories are not just told, but consumed – read, heard, watched, bought … Often this very consumption is closely and directly linked to production: we consume stories in order to produce our own; we produce stories in order to consume them.
>
> (1995, p. 43)

In conducting a focus group, I was able to get at how these 'sexual stories' were exchanged between participants and how they were received. This allowed me to gain insight not only into what happened during their erotic role-play sessions but also how each player's' action was interpreted and 'keyed' (Goffman 1974) by the others.

Additionally, there is past precedent for conducting focus groups with tabletop role-players. Sherry Turkle reported success with having informal 'pizza parties' with role-players in the Boston area (1994). She writes that the richest data she collected was through these meet-ups where she would simply ask players what was on their mind. The format of these focus groups influenced my decision to provide snacks and soft drinks for players during observations and the focus group. Additionally, the success with the casual format used by Turkle influenced the focus-group discussion guide by keeping the questions as open-ended as possible. Asking open-ended questions such as "How do you define erotic role-play?" allowed the participants to use their own definitions, language, and meanings grounded in their own experience to describe specifically how they viewed the activity and what meanings they gave it. Each question in the focus group was related to one of the key research questions. An example of this follows below.

- Research question: What are the crossover effects from sexual play in the game world to sexual play in a player's everyday life?
- Focus group questions: Do you have a partner in real life?
  - How do they feel about your erotic role-playing in the game?
  - Do you think it affects your relationship?

Notes were taken with a pen and pad of paper during the focus group, which helped recall hand gestures, facial expressions, and body language. These notes were useful in analysis as they helped to indicate the tone and mood of the group when certain topics were discussed. For example, the overall tone of the focus group was humorous, with participants smiling and laughing throughout. However, when Dan recounted his favourite erotic role-play experience, in which his favourite character committed suicide, the group became quiet and stopped smiling. By noting that participants' body language changed, with Joe and Scott looking down at their hands, I was able to note the mood markedly changed from joyous to sombre, which added gravity to Dan's retelling of his experience.

INTERVIEWS WITH *WORLD OF WARCRAFT* PARTICIPANTS

As briefly mentioned earlier in this chapter, I had entered the field as a researcher by creating a profile on the guild's web forum with links to my university web page. During early stages of observation, I realised the guild's forums were regularly read by members. It therefore seemed a logical place to post a call for participation and recruit participants for the interview phase of the research.

I created two identical forum posts, placing one in a public area viewable by all members of the guild and the other in an age-restricted area. The public-area post was created so all guild members would know my character and I were in the guild to conduct research and what the research entailed. The post additionally contained contact information for potential participants to volunteer to be interviewed. I asked that all potential participants contacted me privately, either by a private message on the forum, in-game, or via e-mail. A second forum post, identical to the first, was placed in a special section of the forums only visible to guild members with a registered forum account who had proven themselves to be over the age of eighteen to the guild leaders and forum moderators. This area of the forum was dedicated to discussion, art, fan fiction, and role-play with mature topics and primarily dealt with erotic role-play. Throughout fieldwork, I occasionally updated the forum posts for secondary calls for participation and to notify members when the fieldwork had ended.

Using individual interviews in the place of focus groups worked well for *World of Warcraft* participants as the guild is rather large and many players stressed the importance of privacy and anonymity online, even amongst friends. In practical terms, the interviews were conducted using a private chat function embedded in the game that allows for a private conversation between two players. The interviews were recorded using an add-on entitled Elephant, a modification to *World of Warcraft's* code developed by third-party designers. Through Elephant, chat is viewed and recorded in a separate window from the game's in-built chat. The add-on additionally allows users to copy and paste text, which cannot typically be done through the game's built-in chat system.

I initially found out about Elephant through participants' recommendation and use. It was widely used within the guild to record minutes of guild meetings and was widely used by participants to record and store their favourite erotic role-play sessions for later reading. As a research tool, it proved to be useful in eliminating transcription but it did present an interesting ethical problem later in the research. After an interview, a participant sent me an Elephant-recorded chat log between her and her erotic role-play partner. Initially I was elated at the opportunity to read and analyse an example of an erotic role-play session, and she was happy to provide me with the example. However, her erotic role-play partner was not a member of the guild or a participant in the study, and thus had probably not seen the posted information about the study and had not read or signed the informed consent. Before reading the log, I thought carefully about ways around the ethical dilemma it presented and considered approaching the other player and asking if they would like to participate in the study. However, approaching this player would not only reveal their partner was participating in the study, a breach in confidentiality in itself, but could also potentially cause problems between the participant and the other player. If the other player was not aware their partner had recorded the log or had sent it to a researcher, they might lose trust in their partner. It was a difficult decision to make but ultimately I deleted the chat log.

The interview questions were designed in much the same way as those for the tabletop focus group and closely followed the original research questions. They were also open ended and designed to get at the experience of erotic role-playing. For example, one question asked participants to recount their favourite erotic role-play session and explain why it was their favourite. This question not only allowed for insight into what is actually done in erotic role-play but also how the participants themselves framed it within their own lived experiences. This question in particular yielded deep, rich data that demonstrated the interactions between discourse and rules, what constitutes good erotic role-play, and how the participants themselves experienced and interpreted the act into a narrative of their own sense of a sexual self.

The questions were also designed to get at a particular aspect of the research objectives. For example, in order to understand if rules influenced role-play and if so, which ones and how, I asked participants if there had ever been a sexual situation in the game in which they, as a player and a person, felt uncomfortable. If they had, a follow-up question asked if they were able to manage the situation. Asking about a specific experience prompted participants who had experienced an uncomfortable situation to think about their personal or communal boundaries, limits, and rules that they felt were crossed. This additionally prompted an explanation of how social rules within the erotic role-play community are enforced and what resources are used in the enforcement. To take into account the observed forum use, an additional question asked about participants' creation of erotic art and fiction. Although not every participant posted erotic stories or artwork on the forums, some did, and they were asked about the themes present in the work as well as their motivation to create it.

ETHICS AND PARTICIPANT-RESEARCHER RELATIONSHIP

The two foremost limitations that affected this study are 'going native' and 'role conflict'. Going native is an anthropological term concerning the loss of a researcher's objectivity when deeply imbedded among a group of participants (Paccagnella 1997). I counter this as a concern by arguing that since this research began through my own experiences of role-playing within the studied communities, there was little objectivity to begin with. Rather than view this as problematic, I adapted the research design to account for my role as a member of the communities being studied. By adopting an epistemological perspective, which treats experience as data and accounts for the role of the researcher in generating and interpreting data, the methodology has been structured to account for an active, subjective researcher. Support for this additionally comes from feminist research methodologies. As Timothy Diamond writes, "If there are stories, there has to be an author/researcher active in their production; there's no room in this method for an invisible researcher" (2006, p. 59). In this case, the epistemology accounts for subjectivity and a visible researcher presence as part of the research methodology.

The second issue to contend with, role conflict, refers to an incongruity between the goals of the group and the goals of the research project wherein the researcher feels torn (Paccagnella 1997). Because I identified myself as a member of the communities studied, role conflict was a particularly important concern. If my emotional attachment to participants led to misrepresentation, it could not only hurt my relationship with the role-playing communities studied but also affect the reliability, quality, and robustness of the data. To manage this, I employed practical strategies to record and manage my feelings towards participants and recall the specific circumstances under which the data was collected. Throughout the nine months of fieldwork, I kept a research diary in which I would note what I accomplished that day, particular themes of interest that had come through observation, and my in- and out-of-character interactions with participants.

At several points during the fieldwork, I noted events that, embedded in the research process or not, affected me emotionally. In the weeks preceding the focus-group interview, one of the tabletop participants found out he had been exposed to HIV. Although it did not come up during the focus-group interview, he had spoken to me beforehand to let me know he was undergoing a peptide treatment to try to stop the infection. The treatment, the physical side effects, and the mental and emotional side effects undoubtedly affected the group as a whole, including myself. I felt a mixture of sympathy, depression, and helplessness as I witnessed his struggle for health.

Additionally, the research was conducted during a time of an economic recession, which affected participants' lives in very direct ways. During the fieldwork, several of the *World of Warcraft* participants expressed financial worries, with some having to pause their subscription to the game to prioritise bills over the monthly game fee. It was emotionally difficult for me to read participants' accounts of financial problems and this had a direct effect on the methodology. I had originally planned to meet the online participants in-the-flesh at BlizzCon. I had intended to pay for the participants' entry fee to the convention as a reward for their participation, as well as an incentive to conduct a follow-up interview or focus group once there. However, it became quickly apparent that offering to pay the entrance fee to a convention that required travel and accommodation costs was not only impractical, it was also insensitive to the participants' financial struggles. With several members suffering economic hardships, I instead decided to reward participants with a month-long subscription to the game.

Role conflict also led to ethical problems concerning my dual roles as researcher and participant. As a researcher, I felt the need to at least attempt to treat each participant with professional courtesy, which was not always easy. One participant in particular made this process quite difficult with the way she played her character. The character was a well-established elder within the guild's ranks and had a particular dislike for my character's personality. No matter how often I tried to avoid this character in role-play, she would inevitably find my character and bully her. I chatted often to the player out-of-character and developed a friendship with her, yet her character's behaviour was a constant annoyance. Eventually the character died in the apex of a lengthy and intricate plot within the guild and I, out-of-character, actually felt happy. And then I felt guilty. Celebrating death, even of a fictional character, felt both unprofessional and immoral. Reflecting on my emotions, along with the writings of Kathy Charmaz, led to the realisation that as long as I still respected the player, I could continue with the research and include this participant's interview in the data set. Charmaz writes:

> Respecting our research participants means acknowledging and honouring their fundamental humanity. It means treating people with

dignity when we do not condone their beliefs and actions. It also means searching for their meanings and understanding their actions as they see them, not according to our philosophical or professional perspectives.

(2004, p. 985)

In order to understand the character's actions as the player saw them, I needed to search for the meanings she attributed to those actions. The above quote served to remind me that although the character was acting in a particularly unfriendly way, the player meant the actions within the context of role-play. Additionally, experiencing real, out-of-character distress from in-character interactions gave me insight into the very human interactions taking place through a computer-mediated game. It caused me to pause and reflect on how interactions between characters will often affect the players behind those characters, which is instrumental in understanding the many nuances involved in role-playing.

My sometimes mixed feelings towards participant-characters were not the only ways in which my role as researcher was tested. Wanting to minimise potential distractions that my fieldwork might have caused for players not participating in the study, I had initially designed my character to appear as neutral and asexual as possible. The main justification for doing this was to appear to be impassive in discussions of sexuality. I wanted participants to feel comfortable and not to feel they would be judged personally when discussing erotic role-play with me. I created a Blood Elf holy priest. As the class title implies, holy priests are modelled after Western interpretations of Christianity, complete with a focus on modesty and chastity. Additionally, I chose to dress the character modestly, having her prefer to wear the plain robes of her spiritual order. During the role-played interactions of fieldwork, my character initially relied on her role as a priestess to present herself as chaste and abstinent for spiritual reasons. This initial form of self-presentation not only had a distancing effect through the character's rigidity about her spirituality but also I somehow failed to notice role-playing a priestess and then asking participants to discuss erotic role-play in interviews with me was much like a form of Catholic confession and this might achieve the opposite of the intended effect and make participants feel as though they were being judged.

Another ethical issue I had hoped to avoid by creating the chaste priestess character was one of disclosure. I was concerned that openness about my personal beliefs regarding erotic role-play would skew what participants were willing to tell me for fear of judgement. In order to remain open to participant responses, I had initially decided to limit how much of my personal views emerged by refusing to answer personal questions until the interview or focus group had finished. What I discovered, however, was that participants were actually much more eager to share their experiences after I had shared my own. This sharing was accomplished not only through participant observation and my character's development through role-play[9], in which in- and out-of-game sexuality was often a topic of group discussion, but also through reading and commenting on forum posts. Rather than consider my character's social development a conscious methodological decision made at the time of fieldwork, I feel as though it emerged organically from role-playing with participants. Looking back on how I initially entered the field, however, I now see my attempts at limiting personal involvement and expression were not only inconsistent with the rest of the epistemological framework but also hindered partici-pant responses.

Other researchers have experienced similar results. For example, whilst conducting interviews for her graduate work on the wives of clergymen, sociologist Janet Finch was unsure whether she should disclose to her participants that, like them, she too was at the time married to a vicar. After she did, she recounts:

> The consequence was that interviewees who had met me at the front door requesting assurances that I was not going to sell their story to a Sunday newspaper or write to the bishop about them, became warm and eager to talk to me after the simple discovery that I was one of them. Suspicious questions about why on earth anyone should be interested in doing a study of clergymen's wives were regarded as fully answered by that simple piece of information.
>
> (Finch 1996, p. 172)

Disclosing personal information about past in-character relationships to my participants not only helped them to understand why I was conducting the research but also helped to minimise potential suspicions that the research was being conducted for disingenuous reasons, such as to report the findings to Blizzard's disciplinary committee. For many ethnographers focusing on the power relationships between researcher and respondent, the issue of transparency is an important one. When studying how gay men utilise chat rooms, researcher John Edward Campbell reflected on a similar experience in his fieldwork. He writes:

> This instance is indicative of the sexual tensions underlying the negotiation of power between myself as both researcher and community member and those participating in this study. It became evident at points that there were unexpressed contentions over who dictates whether an online interaction will be a serious interview or flirtatious encounter. At other times, there were significantly deeper emotional (and erotic) tensions underlying interviews, tensions originating from the history I shared with a particular subject.
>
> (2004, p. 40)

Campbell asks how we, as researchers, can ask participants to be open and honest with details of their daily lives if we are not willing to do the same. I found that despite my initial concerns over influencing data and exposing personal aspects of myself, answering participants' personal questions and sharing my own experiences during fieldwork assisted in the collection of rich data. Additionally, I found the majority of participants asked questions that sought validation for their own behaviours or asked questions designed to spark a conversation about shared interests rather than to start a relationship or exploit aspects of my personal life.

The final methodological and ethical concern to be discussed is anonymity. Because of the online component of the research methodology, anonymity presented both a methodological and an ethical issue. Online, in-game interactions do not require users to be in close physical proximity, meet face-to-face, or use web cameras or microphones to communicate, so players of *World of Warcraft* are provided with a type of anonymity not afforded to the tabletop group. Whereas tabletop role-players need to meet face-to-face to play, and thus disclose their location and physical characteristics, *World of Warcraft* players had greater control over how much personal information about their real self they gave out to other players. In theory, the anonymity of *World of Warcraft*'s medium meant players could choose to misrepresent themselves.

This uncertainty about real identity has posed methodological problems for past online research. To verify their participants were who they claimed to be, Sherry Turkle (1995) and T.L. Taylor (2006) met their online participants in-the-flesh. I attempted to do this as well, but as detailed above, was in practice unable to do so. Other researchers, however, have pointed out how verifying participants in the real world somewhat undermines the point and purpose of virtual ethnographies. Commenting on this in relation to his own research into chat rooms, Campbell gives two epistemological ramifications for meeting online participants in-the-flesh:

> First, it imposes geographic restrictions on a space in which the lack of a physical topography is such a unique and important characteristic. Second, and perhaps more important, it implies that the online persona is distinct from and less valid (less 'real') than the offline person. ... this distinction between the offline person (the body in the physical world) and the online persona (the self interacting in cyberspace) is fundamentally flawed.
>
> (2004, p. 44)

Campbell makes the point that not only does meeting in-the-flesh undermine an important aspect of the nature of the research, the interest in studying computer-mediated interactions, but also it presumes a clear distinction between offline and online. In using offline meetings as a form of verification, there is an inherent and unfair presumption that online participants are not portraying their true selves and this does not occur in offline research. As detailed in this chapter, Gary Alan Fine (1983) found tabletop role-players who met in the real world rarely shared personal details, such as surnames, with one another. Likewise, offline research more often than not relies on participants to tell the truth without secondary verification. For example, an in-the-flesh interviewer who asks a participant's age might be able to judge the validity of their response by appearance, but rarely are secondary documents, such as a birth certificate or passport, asked for. Thus although participants in virtual worlds may in some ways be more anonymous than their offline counterparts, there is no methodological need or epistemological reason within this study to ask for secondary verification.

Due to the private and sensitive nature of erotic role-play, the anonymity of players was an ethical concern throughout the research. At no point were birth or legal names used in the recording of data. Participants were only required to sign the informed consent. E-mail addresses were used in place of a signature for the online *World of Warcraft* participants. Details that could possibly be used to identify the participants, either online or offline, such as guild name, character name, detailed character descriptions, or physical descriptions of players were not recorded. Character names or online 'handles' "can prove to be a profoundly personal aspect of an interactant's identity ... and needs to be treated with due care by the researcher. Unlike offline names which are generally assigned at birth and used in public interaction, online nicknames function as mode of self-expression in textual spaces" (Campbell 2004, p. 48). Indeed, there is a great importance placed on creating a character name that both fits with the role-play setting and is unique and recognisable to a single individual. In the place of birth or character names, I asked participants to choose their own pseudonyms. Asking participants to create their own pseudonyms served the purpose of allowing the self-expression and identity work that goes into character names to emerge without a threat to the participants' anonymity. Additionally, this allowed the name to still have meaning for the individual participant. As a result, many of the pseudonyms that appear, such as Old Dirty Troll, are both unique to the study as well as expressive of an aspect of the participant's identity. If a participant did not have a preference, I randomly assigned a pseudonym.

My decision to keep respondents' on- and offline identities private was supported and rewarded during the focus group with tabletop players. When discussing the group's perceived differences between online and offline erotic role-play, the topic of online anonymity was brought up. Dan mentioned how he had been fairly notable within a small community of players in a multi-user dungeon and how, through a casual in-the-flesh conversation at a pub, it was revealed that many of the friends he had made online were in his same offline social circle. This example, printed in full in Chapter Four, makes clear the importance of keeping even character names anonymous.

NOTES

1. See for example Valenti, J. (2009). *The Purity Myth: How America's Obsession with Virginity is Hurting Young Women*. Seal: Berkley, CA.
2. Further description of this is found in Chapter Four.
3. Unfortunately, *The Dragon* moved to an online format in 2007 and demographic records of subscribers are either no longer collected or not made available to the public.
4. Not all MMORPGs require a subscription fee but many do.
5. This is to say, unlike tabletop role-players, who are a difficult population to locate, there are several online communities, such as forums set up to support MMORPG players, which facilitates calls for participation in research.
6. As detailed later in this chapter, all participant names have been anonymised through the use of pseudonyms.
7. Here, the term 'primary' makes reference to my uncertainty if other tabletop players would also participate. Joe, Scott, and Dan formed a core group of regular role-players who would take turns at dungeon mastering/storytelling. Occasionally, they would invite friends to temporarily drop in for a session or a campaign.
8. I take the terms 'natural' and 'real-life' from Mason's quote to reference the social reality of playing in virtual worlds, rather than to strictly mean life outside the game.
9. It is important to note that through role-played interactions with the guild, my character's personality changed and developed. Through social events, such as the previously mentioned hen night, her staunch religious views relaxed, she became more sociable, approachable, and relatable to other characters and much more fun to play.

4 Multiple Frames

This chapter is divided into three sections, each representing a theoretical theme that helps to explain the intricacies of the relationship participants have to the types of erotic play they include in their games[1].The first of these research themes concerns the nature of play. In order to understand how the often difficult topics of non-normative sexuality and gender expressions enter games, we must understand game play as different from behaviour. To do this, I will use interview and focus-group excerpts and observations that touch on participants' sexual acts and gender expressions in- and out-of-game. Accompanying these excerpts will be my interpretation and analysis, which relies heavily on Gary Alan Fine's (1983) interpretation of Erving Goffman's frame analysis (1974). Through looking at the multiple frames participants inhabit during game play, illumination is provided on how games provide a distance between the frame of person, player, and character.

Next, the chapter will investigate the various reasons participants gave for erotic role-playing with non-normative sexual acts and expressions of gender. In order to more completely answer the primary research question, and to understand the phenomenon in a way consistent with the epistemology, participant justifications and reasons for erotic role-playing are included in their own words. These responses are then interpreted using two research themes: bounded space and discourse.

The concepts in bounded space are built from an amalgamation of the theories already mentioned in Chapter Two ,which argued games and play provide a space that is marked as different from players' everyday lives and behaviours. This section relies on the already familiar works of Johan Huizinga (1949) and Roger Caillois (1961) to describe play and games as providing a space for the exploration of non-normative themes. Through play's difference from everyday behaviour, in that actions done in play are 'keyed' (Goffman 1974) as being done in jest or for fun, play is viewed as a relatively safe space to express behaviours that would otherwise be socially unacceptable in the players' everyday lives. For erotic role-players, this idea is extrapolated upon and the argument is made that the nature of play allows for non-normative sexual themes and expressions of gender to emerge in erotic role-play because players have recourse to claim their acts were done in jest or just for fun.

Taking my approach, which combines insights from Foucault and play theory, we can explore the issue of the interaction of sexual behaviour with knowledge and power through the third theoretical concept: discourse. Foucault (1978) defines discourse as the dissemination of knowledge and power that shapes how individuals view themselves as ethical subjects in relation to their sexual behaviour. The responses here focus largely on how the bounded space of games allows for different expressions of sexuality to emerge based not on material realities of participants' everyday lives but on the possibilities offered by a tactical distancing of the self from the character. It is argued this tactical distancing, as occurs in play, additionally distances the player from the sexual discourses that structure ethical sexual behaviour in the real world from the discourses present in the game world. This lateral shift in discourse represents a shift in the ethical framework of subject-constitution which, along with the bounded space of games, allows for non-normative sexual behaviours to be experimented within erotic role-play.

The ethnographic data of the chapter and the three theoretical interpretations come together finally at the conclusion. By understanding players inhabit multiple frames of experience during play, and play provides a bounded space wherein difficult concepts may be played with, a rich and descriptive answer to the primary research question is given. Through an understanding of erotic role-play as providing a space to play with non-normative sexuality by virtue of its distance from normative sexual discourse and the self, a complete picture of how erotic role-play provides a space for experimentation with gender and sexuality is formed.

MULTIPLE FRAMES

Participants' responses to the interview and focus-group question 'Describe your character's gender and sexuality. Is it similar or different from your own?' and supporting data from observations are interpreted using Gary Alan Fine's (1983) take on Erving Goffman's frame analysis (1974). Key to this section is the idea participants experience erotic role-play through either the character/diegetic frame or the player frame and not through the primary social frame. This not only answers the primary research question in demonstrating erotic role-play is used to experience non-normative sexuality but also provides insight into how it is done. The interview and focus-group excerpts show how participants were able to inhabit multiple frames of experience during erotic role-play that allowed for non-normative erotic themes to emerge from a distancing of the participants' sense of self and the ethical codes present in the primary social frame.

To begin, many responses to the interview and focus-group question asking players to describe their character's gender and sexuality focused on the differences between player and character. In some responses. differences were explained as emerging through play as a part of character and story development. In one such example, Rasha wrote, "The only thing [my character and I] have in common is the preference for women". When asked why this is, she responded, "Character forging". The term 'character forging' is a metaphor for the building and development of a fictional character similar to the forging of a sword over an anvil. It makes reference to the laborious process undertaken by role-players to develop and shape their characters into deeply complex creatures with their own tastes and preferences. Additionally, in Rasha's quote, she points out that although she and her character have a preference for women, that's where the similarities end. The sexual activities player and character enjoy are quite different.

Other respondents focused on the differences between their sexual preferences and that of their characters as stemming from unfulfilled desires in their sexual routine. In one example of this, two participants discussed how they used erotic role-play to satisfy desires they were uncomfortable with in-the-flesh. *World of Warcraft* players Megan and Caleb have been in a monogamous relationship for over ten years. They are in their late twenties and live in Canada. During my observations I noted Megan and Caleb each had multiple unique characters they erotic role-played with, and each of Megan's characters was paired with one of Caleb's. Although they usually erotic role-played exclusively with one another, upon occasion they would involve a third party either in-game or in a story that would then be posted on their guild's forums. An excerpt from one of their co-authored stories is included below.

> Sometime later the three of them lay there atop the dishevelled bed, sprawled about, though altogether. [Character 1] and [Character 2] both were silently still, curled into [Character 3's] sides, their arms reaching across his broad chest in the trio's silence.
>
> (Excerpt from an erotic story by Megan and Caleb)

During the interview with Megan and Caleb, I asked about the inclusion of a third party in their erotic role-play and whether or not this reflected part of their in-the-flesh sex. Their responses, which follow, detail how they view the separation between their and their characters' sexual preferences and why they include the themes they do in their erotic play.

> MEGAN: I find other women attractive (though I haven't found another man attractive, physically, in a long time), but real sex, well … there's real concerns. Like emotional attachment, diseases, hurt feelings, etc. In *WoW*, those problems are manageable.
>
> CALEB: Yes, likewise to Megan. I have no objection to the notion of sex with another man, but it's never been something I've done, or have any real desire to. I, quite frankly, don't really have a desire for sex with anyone but Megan in real life. My mind tends not to work that way.

INTERVIEWER: And yet your mind works that way in *WoW*?

CALEB: Yes. When I'm in the mindset of my character, it could be completely driven to have more sexual partners, to lust for others or whatever.

MEGAN: Besides, if we were to have another person join us in bed, we'd probably have to clean up the apartment. And I figure, if a threesome can't get me to clean the apartment, I probably don't want it that bad.

CALEB: Plus, in real life the sexually transmitted disease warnings as a kid totally traumatized me for life. I see anyone I might have any sexual interest in as a potential disease box.

In the interview responses, Megan and Caleb touch upon both their desire to involve a third person in sex and the practical downsides to an activity that sounds romantic and intimate in their fictional stories. In the opening quote from Megan, she mentions that although she is in a monogamous relationship with a man (Caleb), she finds other women sexually appealing and implies she would enjoy sex with Caleb and another woman if it weren't for perceived risks associated with the behaviour. Likewise, Caleb responds that although he does not take issue with involving a third in their relationship, he only desires Megan in real life. Importantly, Caleb makes the distinction that when he is in the mindset of his character, it is possible the character could develop a desire for another. I interpret Caleb's responses as representative of the multiple frames of experience that players occupy during game play.

Using Goffman's idea of frames, Fine simplified the many frames at work during a role-play session by picking out three levels of meaning. Recalling the list in Chapter Two, he lists them as the primary social frame, the secondary player frame, and the third character/diegetic frame[2]. Two of these frames are present in the interview excerpt. As people, Megan and Caleb occupy the primary social frame in their discussion of the practical downsides to bringing a third person into their real-life sexual activities. They, somewhat humorously, ground their justifications for not including a third by pointing to both normative behaviour associated with courtship and to warnings of promiscuity present in medical discourse on sex. Megan's realisation that having a threesome in real life would require her to clean the apartment is indicative of the importance she places in the symbolic presentation of home environments as a careful presentation of the self (Goffman 1959). The desire for a threesome is trumped for Megan by what she feels is a necessary tidying of her home. I read this necessary tidying as connected to both Megan's earlier comment and Caleb's follow-up comment regarding sexually transmitted disease. In presenting the apartment as clean, they would be symbolically representing themselves as having a clean bill of health. The focus on both cleanliness and medical discourse relating to sex will be picked up later in this chapter. For now, the diegetic frame will be discussed.

The diegetic frame involves the concept of diegesis, or the game world as experienced by characters (Fine 1983; Montola 2008). Rather than viewing potential character actions in terms of physical possibility in the real world, character actions are viewed within their own context, within their own worlds. I use the diegetic frame to help interpret the part of Caleb's response that outlines the shift from his mindset to his characters'. In Caleb's primary social frame he has no desire to break his monogamy with Megan. However, in his diegetic frame, in which he experiences his character's world through his character, monogamy is negotiable. This is not to suggest Caleb completely abstracts himself from his character – as we know, "in conversations, people slip and slide among frames" (Fine 1983, p. 183) – but rather that he acts within a different frame of experience, one that is distanced from the primary social frame during play. In order to illuminate further how non-normative sexuality and gender enters role-play, additional examples are needed.

The next example, also taken from an interview with a *World of Warcraft* participant, provides further evidence that the sexuality present in erotic role-play differs from the participant's real-life, normative sexuality. Importantly, this interview excerpt supports the claim that erotic role-players experiment with non-normative themes in their erotic role-play. The following excerpt comes from my interview with Cog. Cog is a woman originally from California in her late twenties currently living with her Canadian spouse in Canada. She professed an interest in writing fiction and took great pride in the creative development and penning of her characters. She frequently posted erotic stories about her primary character's sexual activities on the forums. When I asked if she could describe her character's gender and sexual preference and whether or not it differed from her own, she responded that her character was very different.

> COG: She's definitely more … what's the word? [Character] was very primal. She saw, she liked, she took. She was very in the moment. I'm quite shy sexually. I have all these ideas and thoughts in my head but the trick is to express them. [Character] was very open.

During the interview, I asked if Cog would share her favourite erotic role-play session with me so I could get an idea of what she meant by primal. I read Cog's retelling as indicative of the multiple frames of experience occurring during role-play. Her description of what happened to her character is told from the frame of player. At several points in her description, however, she uses parenthesis to insert additional information she recalls from her primary social frame. The separation between the player frame and primary social frame helps the idea that the actual event happened in the diegetic, interior worldview of the game come forward.

> COG: The first part [her character and another] had been instigating each other to no end and finally they took off. Departing company

in frustration only to run into each other again (totally random run in as well) they basically dry-humped in the streets of the [city]. He drugged her, carried her off. He drugged her so that she could explain to her husband that she was drugged and didn't do it of her own accord. She calls rape having *just* gotten clean from drugs and whatnot. People come, separate the two. Not a week later he finds her in [different city] (again, totally random). They talk, they walk. They instigate. He shoves her against a tree and it had to be the most (this sounds odd) passionate, heated, incredibly hot role-play that seriously spoke to what was going on between the two characters. (Emphasis original)

The way in which Cog retells her favourite erotic role-play experience, as well as the content within the retelling, provides insight into how she switches between frames even when recounting the story. Her use of parenthesis to include additional information about how she viewed the role-play as 'totally random' and her descriptions might sound 'odd' not only helps to interpret the session and the spontaneity that made it her favourite but also to show the session was experienced in multiple frames. Although the act took place within the diegetic frame, Cog discusses it from the player frame through the lack of first-person pronouns. It was not Cog pressed against the tree but rather her character. As she discusses the events that occurred in-game, her parenthetical comments provide insight into how she read the act whilst embodied in her primary social frame. Within the primary social frame, Cog realises her description of her character's encounter as 'passionate, heated, incredibly hot' might sound odd, and so she attempts to provide additional insight into how it should be keyed. As the last sentence of the excerpt reads, the erotic role-play experience occurred 'between the two characters' and not between Cog and another player. Although Cog herself may have found the experience 'incredibly hot', she maintains there is a separation between herself and her character and their behaviour.

As Cog was reflecting on the differences between her and her characters, she brought up the separation between erotic role-play and her in-the-flesh sexual activities. I had asked her if she ever shared her stories or her erotic role-play sessions with her husband, and although she had, he responded with little interest.

> COG: I have discussed it with him, he's come and looked over my shoulder to watch a session or two. Or asked very tongue in cheek who's getting their knickers in a twist now. He's very apathetic towards it. It doesn't affect our daily lives so he has no issue.

When I followed up on her comment stating ERP does not affect her daily life with her husband and asked if she had ever tried any of the activities present in her erotic role-play with him, she responded negatively.

COG: No. I'll be the first to admit I *love* my husband. He's incredible, but our marriage, our relationship as a whole has never been entirely sexual. He likes things how he likes them and I"m perfectly happy just to participate with him. (Emphasis original)

Cog's interview responses reflect similar themes to Megan's and Caleb's. All three participants admit the activities present in their erotic role-play, such as threesomes and public trysts, are not a part of their normal, routine, everyday sexual lives. By including themes not present in their normative sexual routines, all three participants' responses provide insight into how non-normative sex enters their frames of experience through erotic role-play. Additionally, their responses contribute to the current body of literature on the performance of sexuality within online games. As referenced in Chapter Three, current studies on sexuality in games have often overlooked or failed to acknowledge the nuanced separation between frames at play. Unlike Jenny Sundén's blurring of a real-life and in-game relationship (2012) or Tom Boellstorff's participants' claim that sex in *Second Life* is 'sex in virtual places' (2008, p. 160), the interview excerpts above suggest at least some erotic role-players create, manage, and define boundaries between the diegetic experiences of their characters and their experiences of erotic role-playing. Although Cog is full of very creative sexual ideas, she realises the limits of enacting those ideas in-the-flesh. Her husband's disinterest in erotic role-playing and the types of sexuality she might play within the game no doubt assist in keeping her experiences within the diegetic and she reports she is happy with that. Like Megan and Caleb, the non-normative sexuality present in Cog's erotic role-play does not enter her normative routine with her spouse.

Likewise, the tabletop group reported the sexuality of their characters reflected very little of their out-of-game sexuality. Unlike the *World of Warcraft* participants, however, the tabletop role-players did not initially draw on their social or player frames but focused solely on the diegetic in their response. During the focus group, Dan, Scott, and Joe discussed character sexuality as usually emerging during play.

INTERVIEWER: Do you typically play characters of a similar sexual preference to your own?

DAN: Um, it's not one of those things that I typically think about, to be honest. Not while I'm generating a character anyway. Sometimes it will pop up.

JOE: I always figured out sexuality on the fly before. Wasn't it your Tremere[3] that was a fat, gay Nazi that flew around with bolts of lightning?

DAN: [Laughing] Yes, he was a German Tremere who was a pyramid fanatic and had Status, Power of the Pyramid, Movement of the Mind, and, um, Way of the Lightning Bolt Two[4]. So he did just wander around taking pot shots at things with a crossbow and electrocuting people while bellowing orders to all of his little minions. Um, occasionally when it is a core part of a character concept I work out their sexual orientation, or it will just pop into my head as being obvious.

SCOTT: I tend to do it on the fly.

DAN: I know what you mean, but sometimes it just *is*.

Even as Dan states that occasionally a character's sexuality will just 'pop' into his head as being obvious, he still has the overall story and how the character's sexuality will fit within that story in his mind. I read his response, and Scott and Joe's responses of figuring sexuality out 'on the fly', as similar to Rasha's 'character forging'. It is a part of the framed experience of role-playing. As the focus group continued, I pressed the group to more thoroughly describe past characters' sexuality in relation to their own.

SCOTT: Many of the characters I've played have either hedged around sexuality or they have been straight anyway, which is kind of different from me because I'm not!

JOE: My elf was straight, the first character I ever played, but it never really came up. Uh, the wizard was bi[sexual], although he really tended to go after Paul's hot cleric because we were actually dating at the time.

SCOTT: Oh, you should never sleep with your boyfriend in-character.

JOE: [Chuckles]

DAN: No, that's just bad. [Mocking voice] Well, at least our characters are doing it!

JOE: Ugh, that sadly is so true.

INTERVIEWER: Wait, what? Can you repeat that?

JOE: Sorry, what he was saying was that it seems such a shame that we're not getting to have sex, but at least our characters do. That is usually the case when–

SCOTT: It is always upsetting when one of your characters has a better sex life than you do!

JOE: Yeah, when you role-play with your partner, you often find that you've segregated off your sex life and you just role-play.

In the second comparison of erotic role-play and in-the-flesh sex, the tabletop group discussed not only playing characters with different sexual preferences but also the overlap between character and player experience. In Joe's discussion of a time when he had a bisexual character with an interest in his boyfriend's character, he mentions the role-play took precedence over their actual sex life. Scott and Dan jokingly point out it is upsetting when characters have a more active sex life than the players do. The relationship between players' sexuality and their characters' sexuality is often neglected in studies on tabletop gaming. In Gary Alan Fine's ethnographic account (1983), for example, male characters were noted as treating female characters as property or sexual objects but analysis on the relationships between players' sexuality and their characters', or even players' political beliefs about the treatment of women, was not included. In addition to providing insight into how characters' sexuality is either chosen or developed in tabletop gaming, Dan, Scott, and Joe additionally provide insight into how characters' sexuality relates to their own out-of-game relationships. I interpret these comments as both being indicative of the time-consuming nature of tabletop role-playing and of the differences between the frames of self and character.

As previously noted by Fine (p. 63), tabletop role-play is a notoriously time-consuming activity, with sessions lasting eight hours or more. This was the case for the tabletop participants in this study, who would meet once a week on Sunday and spend between six and eight hours role-playing. The required time commitment had an effect on the personal relationships of the participants, as evidenced in the previous focus-group excerpt. My notes from around the time of the focus group stated Dan, Scott, and Joe were without significant others, but this was not always the case. Joe mentions his boyfriend Paul's character during this part of the focus group. I learned during observation that Paul's presence in that particular campaign was his first and last time role-playing. Interested in this point, I asked further questions.

Both Joe and Paul work full-time jobs during the week and Paul saw Joe's Sunday role-play sessions as cutting into the quality time they spent together. To spend more time with Joe, Paul joined the group. Perhaps because of Paul's reasons for joining, Joe's character took a particular sexual interest in Paul's. Once their characters began having sex, though, Scott and Dan jokingly point out their in-the-flesh sex stopped. Out of the many ways of interpreting this, I choose to use a similar explanation as I previously employed with the *World of Warcraft* group. The non-normative sexuality expressed by players in games is expressed there, and not in-the-flesh, for a reason. Joe mentions segregating off his sex life with Paul for the sake of role-play. This could either mean they were satisfied from the sex present in the role-play sessions and didn't feel the need to incorporate sex into their lives, or that time constraints led them to choose sex in-game over sex in real life. In both cases, however, it is evident the erotic role-play in games remained there. The conclusion this excerpt and the interviews with Rasha, Megan, Caleb, and Cog lead me to is that experiences made in the diegetic frame tend to remain there.

Much like sexuality, other participants mentioned playing characters of different genders. Emblematic of this is participant Penpy, a married man living in the United States. Penpy was regularly active in all aspects of guild life in *World of Warcraft* and, perhaps due to his nocturnal work schedule, spent a great deal of time creating and developing biographies, histories, and sexualities for each of his ten characters. During our interview he discussed both the gender and sexuality of his multiple characters.

PENPY: Well, technically I consider myself bisexual [in real life], because I find the idea of sexual interaction with both men and women attractive, though I am married to a woman. But my characters have their own preferences. [Female character 1] and [female character 2] are bi. [Male character 2], [male character 3], [male character 1] and [female character 3] are straight, [female character 4] is a lesbian. [Female character 5] is asexual, lol.

At the surface of Penpy's response is the realization that the fantastical nature of role-playing games makes experimentation with varying degrees of non-normative sexuality and expressions of gender easily accessible. While it is possible to create and perform the various gender and sexualities he discusses in the real world, there are significant challenges he would need to face, particularly for someone who is currently invested in a heterosexual, monogamous relationship. If he were to move his playing with multiple expressions of gender and non-normative sexuality into his everyday life, he would likely need to provide several explanations to his family and friends to account for his change in behaviour. However, because Penpy's non-normative expressions happen through characters in the diegetic frame, his wife is likely to brush aside his behaviour as just play. By keeping the non-normative within the diegetic frame, it can be easily excused. In fact, when Penpy was asked to reflect upon his motivation to play characters that occupy the spectrum of sexuality, his justifications focused on the utility of doing so.

In having a range of characters to draw upon and role-play, Penpy could choose which gender and sexuality to employ based upon availability of partners and his mood. The play style of MMORPGs differs from tabletop in a fairly significant way. Whilst the tabletop group has to plan in advance to commute to a physical location at a specific time, erotic role-play in *World of Warcraft* happens much more spontaneously and also much more often. Although some participants, like 33 year-old Greenhat whom we will hear more from later, reported 'booking in' erotic role-play sessions with her partner(s), this was uncommon. Playing multiple characters with multiple sexual preferences allows for a greater chance at successfully finding an available erotic role-play partner.

Like Penpy, other players reported playing characters with multiple genders. One participant even reported playing characters that could switch genders at will. Mocha, a woman in her early twenties living in the United States, spoke about her primary character that she has role-played in many game settings and formats outside *World of Warcraft*. Although she has at least one character in the guild she erotic role-plays with, she said the majority of her ERP encounters, and certainly her favourite, came from entirely text-based sessions on America Online Instant Messenger (AIM). The text-based nature of using an instant messaging service to role-play is perhaps most similar, in environment and format, to the Multi-User Dungeons of the past. In her research into MUDs, Sherry Turkle noted 'gender swapping', or role-playing alternate genders different from a players' real-world gender, allowed players a greater range of emotional expression (1995, p. 222). Although Penpy focused on the utility of having multiple characters with multiple genders and sexual preferences, Mocha hints at the range of experiences such characters afforded her. In her comparison of her own sex life and her character's, she writes:

> MOCHA: [Female character name] (or [male name] when he's male) is my most active and my main character on AIM. He's VERY active, which is the opposite of me. He's pansexual and I'm bi, so there's similarity there. ICly [in-characterly] though he has a lot of fetishes I don't, so I don't play them out.

Much like Cog's contrast between her sexually shy self and her primal character, Mocha is quick to separate herself and her character. Mocha focuses on her character's promiscuity by stating he is 'VERY' active. She positions herself as the opposite of her character in terms of activity. In fact, her sexual orientation is the only similarity she identifies between herself and her pansexual character, even though there is a deliberate distinction between bisexuality and pansexuality. In the real world, Mocha recognizes her attraction to men and women, while her character, following the definition of pansexuality, is open to the possibilities of being attracted to anyone, regardless of perceived gender or sexual identity (Lenius 2001). As a final point, Mocha describes her character as having 'sexual fetishes' she does not share and so she opts out of exploring. In pointing out that her character's fetishes differ from her own, Mocha repeats the key point of this section. Erotic role-play happens in players' diegetic frame during play, and although the players gain the experience of playing with non-normative gender expressions and sexual acts, this experience remains within the diegetic frame. The diegetic and player frames cross very little in terms of employing behaviour used at play in life outside of the game. Because of this, erotic role-play provides a space of minimal risk where non-normative sex can be played with.

This section has presented examples of how non-normative gender and sexuality were played within erotic role-play to answer the primary research question. First, it was established that participants include non-normative sexuality in their erotic role-play through a comparison between reports of participants' ERP and behaviour outside the game. To answer how non-normative gender and sexuality were played with, examples from fieldwork, interviews, and the focus group were interpreted through an analysis of the multiple frames of experience inhabited by participants during play. This helped to demonstrate erotic role-play occurs, and largely remains, in the diegetic frame of experience. The diegetic frame is distanced from players' primary social frame as it concerns only the activities that happen during play through characters. The separation of these frames of experience contributes to a way of thinking about ERP as a bounded game space in which non-normative sexuality can be played with at a minimal risk to the self. In the next section, further examples of non-normative sex in erotic role-play will be provided along with interpretations that rely on the second theoretical theme: erotic role-play as a bounded space.

BOUNDED SPACE

In continuing the exploration of how participants include non-normative sexuality in their erotic role-play, some players discussed using ERP to explore otherwise unknown or uncomfortable themes. Following from Mocha's quote, which ended the previous section, some participants talked about erotic role-play in terms of providing a space within which to experience sexuality. Common in these responses was that the game provides a safe space or a space with manageable risks to try out, experiment, or play with sexuality in a way that is not possible outside the game. I interpret these responses as reflecting erotic role-play's playful and game-like nature.

In one such response Shila, a 41-year-old trans-woman living in the United States, discussed erotic role-play in *World of Warcraft* as providing an outlet for emotional connections between strangers in a safe way. Shila, who works as a live-in caretaker for a family, was single at the time of the interview and expressed difficulties in finding a romantic partner in-the-flesh. She was also undergoing hormone therapy as part of her physical transition to womanhood.

> SHILA: I think that people are craving emotional connections and one of the key elements of MMOs is that they both provide a level of safe distance AND simulate something that approximates face-to-face interactions.

In her response, Shila focuses on the safety offered by the online format of *World of Warcraft* and the potential for establishing emotional connections with other players. She describes social interactions in the game as simulating face-to-face interactions in the real world, which makes connections with past literature and theory on new media. Mark Poster (1995) theorised virtual reality as being a simulation of 'real' reality, which upsets modernist understandings of place as physical. In his view, virtual reality 'duplicates' real reality and also alters it, making "fanciful imaginings that … invoke play and discovery" (1995, p. 30). For Poster, virtual worlds represent a deeper abstraction from reality than text or video in that individuals enter an imaginary world which 'tinkers with reality' (1995, p. 31). In Shila's case, reality is tinkered with through the opening of emotional connections without corresponding feelings of vulnerability that may accompany physical, face-to-face interactions.

I therefore interpret the 'safe level of distance' Shila mentions as referencing physical space and anonymity. Because *World of Warcraft* is a game played on personal computers, players can connect to each other from the perceived safety of their own home without revealing their birth name, face, or any identifying information other than what is evident in the appearance of their character. There seemed to be a common understanding among both *World of Warcraft* and tabletop participants that online space is a safe space because of the anonymity it provides. When I asked what differences, if any, the tabletop players thought there were between the erotic role-play involved in their face-to-face campaigns and those involved in *World of Warcraft*, Scott immediately mentioned anonymity.

> SCOTT: Online will always give you that level of mask and distance. If you say something that makes you look like a tit, by saying you'd like to copulate with a fish on your chest or something, people [offline] are going to stop and look at you funny. Not only that, but they know who you are to point and laugh at in public.

The anonymity provided by role-playing in online formats, however, is limited. Many factors, including character name, description, and style of typing can be used to identify players. Dan was quick to point this out during the focus group in response to Scott.

> DAN: Um, this isn't necessarily true. I mean, when I was Mr. MUD Wizard, my handle, my identity had been preserved across multiple MUDs, it is quite a small community, so I was quite widely known.
> SCOTT: But that's only in that online community.
> DAN: No, it's not. It also bleeds over into the flesh. I mean, I've got some of my close [offline] friends who are also MUDers. They know who I am. I was semi-notable in the small community. So it's not quite as anonymous as you might think.

Aside from these challenges to the claim that anonymity provides a safe distance in role-play, there is a deeper interpretation that can be made. There is another element of distance implied in Shila's quote and this type of distance develops through play. By its nature, play allows for the exploration of sensitive, personal, and uncomfortable issues by providing players with a frame of experience that is distanced from the self. The frivolous nature of play provides players with a rationalisation for characters' actions as being just for fun and not serious. Although to the characters, these actions may be serious and have serious consequences within the diegetic frame, to the players the actions have manageable consequences.

Recalling the second chapter's exploration of the nature of play, Johan Huizinga writes that it contributes to "the formation of social groupings which tend to surround themselves with secrecy and to stress their difference from the common world by disguise or any other means" (1949, p. 13). A reading of this quote might draw attention to the comparisons between the secrecy and anonymity afforded to *World of Warcraft* participants through the online nature of their game, but I believe the secrecy Huizinga references has more to do with the themes involved in play. Support for this reading comes from Caillois' interpretation of Huizinga's quote. He writes, "Without a doubt, secrecy, mystery, and even travesty can be transformed into play activity, but it must be immediately pointed out that this transformation is necessarily to the detriment of the secret and mysterious, which play exposes, publishes, and somehow expends" (Caillois 1961, p. 4). By reviewing Shila's quote within my interpretation of the definition of play, we can see how meaningful emotional connections can emerge through erotic role-play because of its ability to offer a space to explore the mysterious. The mysterious, for the participants in this study, is the non-normative sexuality they employ in their erotic role-play.

To play with sexual practices outside of normalised behaviour sanctioned within a person's primary social frame poses a risk to a person's conceptualisation of an ethical self. By this I mean participants' routine performance of sexuality lacks secrecy and mystery in its pre-exposed and safely sanctioned nature. When performing this type of sexuality, participants are safely cushioned within a pre-negotiated ethical self. Support for this comes from Judith Butler's definition of performativity as being "neither free play nor theatrical self-presentation" (1993, p. 95). Rather she suggests it is "the forced reiteration of norms" (p. 94). When participants use play to explore mysterious and unknown expressions of sexuality, they are breaking away from a forced performance of normative sexuality that poses inherent risks. In exploring the mysterious through breaking away from normative sexual performances, the self is exposed to criticism. This fear of criticism is present in Shila's quote in which she describes craving emotional connections but with a desire to make those connections within a level of safe distance. Likewise, during our interview Megan spoke about how sex is an exposing act and a vulnerable time when I asked if the primary reason she and Caleb erotic role-play was for physical stimulation.

> MEGAN: I'm not sure I'd say primary. I mean, that"s a big reason, but it also comes down to closeness, to exploring things with one another, learning more about one another. And yeah, character development and letting our characters learn more about each other. Sex is a very vulnerable and exposing time for most people, our characters included. We've had some amazing character breakthroughs before/during/after sex.

Megan's choice of words, particularly 'exposing', harkens back to the quote from Caillois. Caillois (1961) describes play as an activity that seeks to expose, publish, and expend secrets and mysteries. Therefore to play with erotic themes outside normal performance is to expose the self to the vulnerability that might result. Games, as a bounded space in which actions are considered to be frivolous and not serious, create a space wherein such vulnerabilities can be managed.

The vulnerabilities exposed in erotic role-play are managed in a variety of ways. The following chapter, which focuses on rules, outlines some of them. Beyond ludic mechanics present in games, however, there are theoretical aspects of play that also serve to bind and limit exposure and vulnerability during erotic role-play. As referenced in the definition of play by Huizinga (1949), the frivolity of play helps to distance the act from the self. I pulled this particular theme out of my interview with Random, a 23-year-old *World of Warcraft* player living in the United States.

> RANDOM: I've heard many stories though of sexual fetishes some RP in, and not my taste [sic]. That of which I won't go into detail, though I'm sure you have some imagination as to how bad some can be. The nature of it varies from person to person, I prefer it to be more warm and cuddly, and sensual, others may be more into it as a pure sake of masturbation [sic]. I see it as an alternative way to strengthen bonds with friends, and just have some silly fun now and again.

Random tells me he has heard stories of some sexual 'fetishes' present in erotic role-play that he finds distasteful and speculates they are done purely for the sake of masturbation. He then goes on justify the erotic role-play he undertakes as a way to socially bond with friends and have some 'silly fun'. I interpret Random's use of the word 'silly' to reference the frivolity present in play. Although other participants, like Cog, mentioned the importance of erotic role-play in developing a narrative between characters, other participants echoed Random's point about silliness and fun.

Initially, the tabletop group stressed that for sex, particularly sexual violence, to enter one of their campaigns, there had to be a diegetic justification. When discussing a time when he was disturbed by a player's insistence that a violent rape happen during a campaign, Dan focused on the importance of character actions fitting with the story. In the focus group, he said, "It's not that I even have any particular problem with it, it's just it needs to have a point and a purpose. In the same way I wouldn't expect a party to stop to break dance". Later in the focus group, however, he relaxed his stance when one particularly silly example was brought up.

> DAN: That's a thought, I say I avoid sex in [*Dungeons and Dragons*], but there was the 'bugger-the-paladin' incident.
> JOE [Points at Scott]: That was his!
> SCOTT: That wasn't entirely my fault, I saved him with a cheese sandwich!

> JOE [Looks Animated]: But you caused it!
> DAN [Laughs]: Yes, you made it happen!
> SCOTT: I stopped it as well!
> Everyone laughs.
> DAN AND JOE: You started it!
> SCOTT: That's not the point, I saved his ass!
> JOE: After getting him buggered.
> SCOTT: Actually, I–
> JOE [Interrupts and Looks at Dan Gesturing to Scott]: Hold your hand
>   over his mouth so he can no longer talk!
> DAN: Actually, you didn't save his ass, you did quite the opposite. You
>   expanded his ass.
> SCOTT: No, I actually didn't touch his ass at all.
> DAN: Anyway–

At the mention of the 'bugger-the-paladin' incident the mood of the focus group changed from a sombre discussion to a humorous and competitive debate as Dan, Scott, and Joe became animated. As evidenced from the excerpt above, they began to talk over one another in rapid succession and as they did so, more examples of the inclusion of frivolous sex in their *Dungeons and Dragons* role-play sessions came forth.

> JOE: There was the incident with the 2 white robes[5] as well. Insert your
>   staff, polymorph!
> DAN AND SCOTT [Laughing]: OH!
> INTERVIEWER: What?
> JOE: They polymorphed[6] the white robe into a hamster whilst he sat
>   on his own staff–
> DAN [Makes an Exploding Gesture with His Hands]: So the hamster
>   went boof!
> JOE [Laughs and Makes a Squishing Noise]: Hamster make a fortitude
>   save[7]. Fortitude modifier is a one, is it?
> DAN [Makes a Squishing Noise]: Minus lots. Hamster's save versus
>   massive damage. Hamster fails.
> INT: So, this player was killed–
> JOE: It wasn't a player. [Dan] created a light[8] party, and they were
>   supposed to smite the smug heroes we had become and Sam's
>   paladin refused to join in the fight–
> SCOTT: He threw a strop.
> JOE: He threw a strop, he couldn't decide whether he should side with
>   his allies or the forces of light, so he sat on the side line and did
>   nothing which lent my neutral[9] character, [Scott's] evil character,
>   the other evil wizard, and the sort of lawful good cleric–
> SCOTT: The very dumb cleric.
> JOE: Yeah, it led to a polymorphed hamster sat on his own staff.

SCOTT: Basically, the moral authority of the party stepped away so we used every method we had available and they lost fast! 'Yay! We don't have a moral authority anymore, we can now be efficient!'

To understand the significance of the retelling of the tabletop group's experience with the polymorphed wizard, we need to understand it from their perspective. Taken on its own, a story of role-played sexual violence could be misinterpreted as having negative implications for the group in the primary social frame. It might be assumed, for example, that sexual violence was used in play to make one or more players feel uncomfortable in their primary social frame, as Fine (1983) observed with male fantasy role-players' treatment of female characters as property. It is in how the story is told, with interspersed laughing, banter, and humorous language, that contextualisation is provided for how such a theme could emerge in play. In Joe's retelling, we see a group of evil characters were confronted by a group of good characters who sought to teach them a lesson in hubris. The evil party, lacking a 'moral authority' to tell them the act was wrong, sought the most 'efficient' way to defeat the wizards of good. Although there are several serious issues in this example, such as good and evil, sexual violence, and moral choice, none of these themes was treated seriously by the participants as each viewed the act as playful. I interpret the way they retold this event to me, their laughing and squishing sound effects, as indicative of the frivolity present in bounded game-spaces.

In my interpretation of this particular example, non-normative sex was played within an exploration of morality, even as it was done with a frivolous tone. Because games offer a bounded space of minimal risk and judgement to the self, over-the-top demonstrations of violence can be included to a humorous effect, and players can push the good/evil dichotomy to extremes. The way in which the wizard was killed pushes on boundaries of acceptability outside the game. However, for those who would argue players engaging in this behaviour have delusions about boundaries of acceptability or do not know what is and is not acceptable, I would point to the deliberate playful nature involved. The tabletop group was only able to play with otherwise serious themes of moral choice and depravity by knowing what constitutes moral and amoral choice. In fact, as the next section outlines, it is through play that a lateral discourse of normativity and acceptability for practical application in games develops.

This section has shown erotic role-play is often used as a way to explore non-normative sexuality within a bounded and safe space. From Shila's interview excerpt, it was learned that some erotic role-players use the activity as a safe way to make emotional connections. The importance of safety was pointed out by Megan in her quote that sex is often a vulnerable and exposing time for people. I interpreted Shila and Megan's statements of safety and vulnerability within theories on play. Through a reading of Huizinga (1949) and Caillois (1961), an understanding was reached that the frivolity of play is a useful tool in distancing play-activities from everyday behaviour.

Because of this distancing, non-normative sexuality can be played within an environment of manageable risks.

In his interview, Random brought forth the idea that erotic role-play can both be about emotional bonds and sensuality and be a silly act of fun. Following from this idea, the tabletop group described one role-play session in which they played with sexual violence and moral choice in an over-the-top, silly way. The tabletop group's toying with boundaries of behaviour and taste helped point out how erotic role-play serves as a bounded space away from the self and normal behaviour. The interview excerpts in this section, and their analysis, show the nuanced nature of erotic role-play in ways absent from the current body of literature on sexuality in games. More complex than Rob Gallagher's documentation of the immature treatment of sex in contemporary digital games (2012), and yet less involved than T. L. Taylor's (2006), Esther MacCallum-Stewart's, and Justin Parsler's (2008) observations of in-character marriages, this section demonstrated how players can use erotic role-play to express non-normative sexuality in serious or silly ways. The next section picks up on ideas of normality and focuses on how play develops its own discourse of sexual normativity.

DISCOURSE AND NORMATIVITY

The third section of this chapter aims to answer how erotic role-players experiment with non-normative sexuality in their role-play by examining ideas of normality inside the game. Part of understanding play as a bounded space requires an understanding that it is, at least in part, abstracted from reality. As detailed in the first section of this chapter, players slip between multiple frames of experience during role-play. From the primary to the diegetic frame, players experience erotic role-play in varying degrees of realness. Their experiences of the possibilities present in game worlds, and how this differs from the possibilities present in the real world, contributes to how non-normative sexuality is played with by actually creating multiple, lateral definitions for what is normative.

During an interview, one player made this point explicit. Grin, a 39-year-old man living in the United States, described the fantasy elements of *World of Warcraft* as contributing to his enjoyment of erotic role-play. In this excerpt from the interview, he describes the role of fantasy as assisting in moving outside 'the bonds of realism'.

> GRIN: Well, breaking outside the bonds of realism with powers, scenarios, races, sizes, forms, species, and more have all been explored by us in our ERP. There have been MANY instances. The mind is powerful in sexuality. It plays a tremendous role and can paint extremely vivid pictures, allowing you to do things

not possible, not socially acceptable, or not literally desirable otherwise.

Referencing back to the previous discussion on the role of frivolity in play to shape a bounded space for the exploration of non-normative sexuality, Grin's quote adds another factor. Besides the actual act of play, the fantasy themes and environments assist in playing with non-normative sexuality by abstracting players out of the 'bonds of realism' and by provoking their imaginations. As Grin says, the mind – or imagination, as I interpret it – affords players the ability to do things 'not possible, not socially acceptable, or not literally desirable otherwise'. The particular phrasing Grin uses is interesting. He mentions the 'not socially acceptable', which I interpret as representing the discourse that informs sexual normativity. Foucault writes that discourse produces sexuality, and that sexuality "is the name given to a historical construct: not a furtive reality that is difficult to grasp, but a great surface network in which the stimulation of bodies, the intensification of pleasures, the incitement to discourse, the formation of special knowledges, the strengthening of controls and resistances are linked to one another, in accordance with a few major strategies of knowledge and power" (1978, pp. 105–6). Likewise, games are different from other media in their separation from reality and this presents users with alternate modes of discourse (Aarseth 1997). Erotic role-play and the playful fantasy environments surrounding it then form an additional strategy of knowledge. Rather than strictly coming from a source of power, however, I interpret the discourse present in erotic role-play as a bricolage of players' frames of experience assisted by the playful nature of games.

From the primary social frame, players enter erotic role-play with an understanding of social acceptability. The understanding of what is and is not acceptable, however, is partially discarded once the player enters the frame of game and of the diegetic reality of their character. The participants in this study, at least, were able to play with non-normative or socially unacceptable themes in the bounded space provided by play. In the previous example of the tabletop group's wizard's death, sexual violence was played with frivolously through the players' understandings of morality within the game's system. Likewise, in the examples that follow, the creativity employed by players in their involvement of non-normative sexuality in erotic role-play reflects knowledge that spans multiple frames. Robert, a 26–year-old *World of Warcraft* player, describes the role of fantasy and imagination in his erotic play.

> ROBERT: It just depends upon the scene and the partner. Everyone is a little different in how 'believable' they want their eroticism to be. I like a little bit of the fantastic, personally.
>
> INTERVIEWER: Why do you like a bit of the fantastic? What does it add?

ROBERT: Well, it's similar to why people role-play in the bedroom. The ordinary can become tedious, and erotic role-play itself is no different. The difference is that in this world and medium, something such as spells and potions exist and can have effects.

Robert compares erotic role-play to offline, in-the-flesh sex by stating both have the potential to become ordinary and tedious. In this instance, he is relying on both his social frame and player frame to make this assertion. The difference that emerges through his comparison is that unlike real life, erotic role-play can escape tedium through the use of ludic mechanics present in the game world. Previous research into games has noted their instantaneous feedback allows for the exploration of discourse and culture through their ludic mechanics, which provide players with the ability to create meaning and investigate cultural meanings embedded in games as they play them (Aarseth 1997; Dovey and Kennedy 2006). Furthermore, it has been noted fans of a particular type of media will often reinterpret or reappropriate content to suit their own cultural understandings, wants, or desires (Jenkins 2006). Robert mentions the use of spells and potions and their effects in such a way. The spells and potions he mentions within *World of Warcraft* are not described as having any sexual function or application. It is the erotic role-players who reinterpret and reappropriate the items and abilities as having sexual use. I interpret participants' appropriation of these items for sexual use as both a play between frames of knowledge and imagination and a subversive and creative development of a form of sexual discourse to suit the needs of players. The knowledge and power of these reappropriated potions and spells represent an active creation of a sexual discourse among erotic role-players that bridges gaps between their framed knowledges. In an example of how these spells and potions are used, excerpts are included below from separate interviews with Mocha and Penpy.

MOCHA: ... me/my rp partner have used things such as telekinetic stimulus, teleporting clothes away, gender-bending, fast-healing for rough sex, etc.

PENPY: I don't think the mechanics play that much into it, unless you're talking about specific class abilities in some fetish play that might come up. I.e. druids using entangling roots ... this game allows for almost limitless possibilities. ... (Ellipses original)

In Mocha's excerpt, abilities that were included in the game for use in battle were reappropriated for use in erotic role-play. Fast-healing spells, which are often a boon to players fighting in lengthy dungeons, can be used to speed up the healing associated with rough sex or sadomasochism. Likewise, in Penpy's excerpt, entangling roots, a druid ability that causes thorny brambles to erupt from the ground and snare a foe, are used as restraints in fetish play. These reappropriations represent player-defined ways of not only developing a sexual repertoire for their characters but also defining sexuality within the game world by defining what is possible. In these ways, a discourse emerges through the formation of special knowledges (Foucault 1978) that is consistent with the literature on games' difference from other textual media (Aarseth 1997; Dovey and Kennedy 2006). In playing with the provided text of the game, erotic role-players develop their own meanings and use of otherwise non-sexualised items. It is in this development of communal meaning for healing spells and potions as aftercare for rough sex, for example, that a lateral discourse emerges for erotic role-play that is separate from institutional discourses about sex. Institutional discourses from the game's developer, which designed healing potions and spells for replenishing hit points lost in battle, and from medical discourse, which cautions against the potentially negative mental and physical health effects of sex, are set aside in favour of a communally developed discourse that defines items and abilities for their use value in erotic role-play. For erotic role-players in *World of Warcraft*, the symbolic meaning of a healing potion or spell or a druid's ability to cast entangling roots becomes quite different from that of a non-erotic role-player or non-player.

In addition to spells and abilities, the setting of the game worlds helped shape the themes and types of sexual expression experienced by erotic role-players. Both the *World of Warcraft* group and the tabletop group played within settings featuring themes present in fantasy literature. During the interviews, several players touched on the appeal of fantasy as a theme and setting and how this contributed to their decision to erotic role-play in a fantasy world. I read these responses as reflecting fantasy as a type of discourse involved in erotic role-play. Two excerpts from separate interviews with Dirty and Priscilla are included below. Dirty is a 34-year-old manager living on the East Coast of the United States, and Priscilla is a 26-year-old student also living in the United States.

> DIRTY: Well I've always had a curiosity about fantasy creatures since I was younger, and my interest in psychology made me really wonder how these things reacted outside of books and games etc. Obviously one of those interactions was relationships and sex, guess I was curious how sex between various creatures would be.
> PRISCILLA: Exotic is exciting. I like the [character] models themselves because they are attractive and pleasing. I've been a fan of fantasy settings since I was very young, so it's fun to role-play in a situation that is otherworldly. I grew up in the SCA and played *D&D* at age 6.

In Dirty's quote, he discusses a curiosity based in fantasy that he developed as a child after reading about fantasy worlds. As has been previously noted, fantasy literature has historically been appropriated for children (Smol 2004;

Prozesky 2006), and thus is typically void of sexual content (Smol 2004). As an adult, Dirty applied his curiosity to the types of interactions and sexual relationships that could develop in such settings. Previous research has noted that one of the attractions of role-playing games is the ability to explore and experience literary fantasy worlds first-hand (Dovey and Kennedy 2006; Barton 2008). However, previous research has failed to provide an in-depth account of how fans of the literary genre may develop a curiosity like Dirty's to explore and play with sexual themes involved in fantasy tropes. In Dirty's account, the absence of sexuality in books and games caused him to wonder about how relationships and sex would function within fantastical worlds.

Like Dirty's interest in fantasy games and books, Pricilla's interest in *Dungeons and Dragons* and the SCA created an interest to role-play in 'otherworldly' situations. The SCA, or Society for Creative Anachronism, is a worldwide organisation that strives to recreate the Middle Ages for fun and entertainment. The SCA is a hybrid existing somewhere between re-enactment and live action role-play, wherein its members loosely recreate a period of history with some elements of fantasy literature but without the existence of magic. What might be thought of as the romantic elements of fantasy, such as costumes, jousts, and chivalric codes of honour, are present. Priscilla references erotic role-playing in a fantasy world as exotic and exciting because of its difference from the everyday world. Additionally, she notes she likes *World of Warcraft's* character models and finds them attractive and pleasing. Priscilla, who drew line art of her Blood Elf character, which will be discussed later, found the elven character models particularly appealing. As previous research has suggested, fantasy's elves are most often associated with femininity and female characteristics (Caldecott 2008; Sundén 2012). They are also often the most highly sexualised in terms of bodily proportions and the design and fit of armour (Taylor 2006). Priscilla's comment about liking the character models themselves becomes particularly interesting when read in conjunction with previous research that suggests although the femininity of elves has often made them the most heavily sexualised fantasy race, sexual acts involving elves are never fully realised in standard fantasy games and literature due to the genre's orientation to child-appropriate themes. In the examples of Dirty and Priscilla, erotic role-players use their specialist knowledge of existing fantasy themes and races and reinterpret them to include sexuality. In doing so, they create a new, specialist discourse for personal use that includes sexual content for fantasy races and characters that may normally be considered child-like and asexual.

So far, this chapter has shown how participants explored non-normative sexuality in erotic role-play by demonstrating the unique discourse of acceptability for sexuality that they develop. This section opened with a quote from Grin in which he stated playing in fantasy games helps the mind break out of realism. I interpreted his quote as making reference to erotic role-play's affordance for players to break out of social norms regarding sex. Rather than view this breaking from social norms as freeform, however,

I note from other interviews that a new discourse develops from a reliance on standard themes and tropes within the fantasy genre. The discourse present in quotes from Mocha, Penpy, Dirty, and Priscilla help to illustrate the sexual discourse for erotic role-players is different from the one present in contemporary, everyday life. The existence of spells and potions and their use as sexual objects in the game, for example, reflect a different set of normative values unique to the *World of Warcraft* participants in this study. The fantasy themes and environments, provided by the bounded game space and experienced through player's multiple frames of experience, contribute to a unique discourse of sexuality in terms of fantasy. In answering the primary research question, while players do play with a type of sexuality in erotic role-play that could be considered non-normative by standards outside the game, inside the game, sexuality is subject to a set of norms created by the players themselves through a reinterpretation of the genre of fantasy and mechanics provided by the game.

CONCLUSION

This chapter aimed to answer the primary research question: Do erotic role-players experiment with non-normative sexuality in their role-play and if so, how? The question was answered by providing examples from participant observation, interviews, and focus-group data. Through my interpretations of the data, it was found participants do experiment with non-normative sexuality through erotic role-playing in games. Further analysis and interpretation explained the nuances of how this was achieved.

The first section discussed examples of how participants' erotic role-play in game environments differed from their out-of-game sexuality. Participant responses from Rasha, Megan, Caleb, Cog, Joe, Scott, Dan, Penpy, and Mocha focused on how few similarities exist between player and character in terms of expression of sexuality and gender. For Megan, Caleb, and Cog, erotic role-play provided a diegetic sexual experience that was undesirable or impractical in their out-of-game sexual routines. For the tabletop group, the decision to develop a character's sexuality was often done with little or no considerations of how it could reflect or exemplify their own preferences. Finally, Penpy and Mocha's interview excerpts demonstrated the behaviours employed in their erotic role-play are grounded within play and do not overlap with their actual experiences. By demonstrating erotic role-play takes place and remains in the diegetic experiences of characters, it was determined a separation between frames occurs during play that allows for themes to emerge that may be uncomfortable in the primary social frame.

Following these themes, the next section focused on play as a bounded space. Through Shila's description of erotic role-play's ability to establish emotional connections in a safe way, the qualities of play as representing an area of manageable risk were uncovered. Furthermore, it was established through Megan's discussion of sex as a vulnerable and exposing time that the principals of play, which aim to explore the mysterious in a not-serious way, contribute to participants' ability to erotic role-play. The quote from Random about erotic role-play being an opportunity for silly fun with friends helped to support this argument. The term 'silly' was taken to signify a similar concept to 'frivolous', in that play is 'nonutilitarian' and 'disinterested' (Sutton-Smith 2001, p. 203) and 'only pretending' (Huizinga 1949, p. 8). Finally, an excerpt from the tabletop group's retelling of a scene in their ERP that involved difficult concepts of sexual violence and moral choice provided further evidence that play allows for fun, frivolous, and silly treatment of otherwise uncomfortable concepts. I interpreted the participants' responses from this and previous sections as indicative of play's ability to distance diegetic actions from the self. This helped to show non-normative expressions of gender and sexuality are able to come through erotic role-play because of the environment of manageable risks play provides.

The final section of this chapter discussed the role of discourse in providing ideas of normativity for the participants. In the opening, I interpreted a quote from Grin describing erotic role-play's ability to open up definitions of social acceptability as a break from normative sexual discourse. Assisting in this interpretation was a quote from Robert in which he suggests the nature of playing in a fantasy world means there are alternate ways of escaping sexual tedium. Interview quotes from Mocha, Penpy, Dirty, and Priscilla were used in an exploration of how erotic role-play offers non-normative ways to experience sexuality through its fantasy setting. The ways in which participants used the fantasy setting, along with the ludic elements of the game, were then interpreted as providing a different form of discourse and normativity to those present in the standard fantasy genre. The following chapter, which focuses on rules, elaborates on how the ludic elements present in the games played by participants helped to shape the types of sexuality they explored.

NOTES

1. This is consistent with the 'abductive research strategy' (Blaikie 2000) and inter-pretivist methodology outlined in this chapter.
2. Whilst Fine (1983, p. 186) uses the term 'character' to reference the frame in which players experience the game world first hand, I prefer Montola's (2008) use of the term 'diegetic', which more descriptively describes the process of viewing and experiencing a game world as the reality of a fictional character.
3. Tremeres are a breed of vampires from the tabletop game *Vampire: The Masquerade*.
4. Status, Power of the Pyramid, Movement of the Mind, and Way of the Lightning Bolt Two are all character abilities or talents that may be purchased for experience points within the *Vampire: The Masquerade* role-playing game. The 'Two'

that follows Way of the Lightning Bolt indicates Dan had purchased two ranks of the ability, making it a stronger attack.

5. 'White robe' refers to a class of magic-users who cast healing spells with assistance from divine powers.

6. 'Polymorphed' refers to a spell cast by magic-users who can shape-shift something into something else. In this example, a wizard is turned into a hamster.

7. A 'fortitude save' is a 20-sided dice roll used to determine whether or not a creature can withstand physical damage to their body.

8. Light, as used here, refers to 'good' characters within the *Dungeons and Dragons* alignment system (Gygax 1978).

9. Neutral, evil, and lawful good are all terms that reference the *Dungeons and Dragons* six-point character alignment system. Characters can be either good, neutral, or evil and either lawful, neutral, or chaotic. This system is used to develop a basic moral compass and personality to role-play with.

5   The Role of Rules

While the previous chapter established the ways in which players incorporated sexuality into their role-playing games, this chapter looks more specifically at the rules used to do so. Rules, as described in Chapter Two, function to limit and shape play into structured games (Suits 2005). Although Suits' definition of rules focuses on their mechanical function in organising play, there is an additional social function as well. Using Goffman's idea of a primary social framework (1974), some researchers have noted players develop their own sets of rules to govern the social aspects of playing. As elaborated upon in Chapter Two, the primary social frame functions in games through the development of exogenous or social 'house' rules (Björk and Holopainen 2003; Montola 2008). Exogenous rules are as necessary to game play as the ludic and mechanical endogenous game rules since they generally dictate expected behaviour outside of the game that inevitably influences the content and themes accessible for play inside it. Additionally, the themes and concepts present in a game's history and lore present themselves as diegetic rules, which dictate acceptable social behaviour for characters. As this chapter will demonstrate, these three types of rules do much to influence the inclusion or exclusion of erotic role-play.

Rules take on an important role for erotic role-play. By defining boundaries of erotic acceptability, rules limit and allow the expressions of erotic behaviour with which the primary research question concerns itself. However, as past research has shown, players rarely accept rules uncritically. In their research on the function of rules in games, Björk and Holopainen (2003) note exogenous rules usually take the form of supplemental house rules, which add or detract limitations on a game's official rules. A secondary aim of this chapter is to assess how players use and adapt official endogenous, exogenous, and diegetic rules to justify, monitor, and guide their erotic role-play. Likewise, a tertiary aim was to explore how players create their own rules to redefine, supplement, or modify the official rules for the inclusion of erotic content. One of the more interesting results of these research aims was the discovery that players want rules for erotic role-play and if no official rules are provided, the players will create their own.

Overall, this chapter makes a contribution towards understanding how erotic role-play is used by players to experiment with sexuality by looking at how rules limit, structure, and provide an entry point for certain types of sexuality in games. The data in this chapter can be seen as contributing towards an understanding of erotic role-play as an expression of sexuality that conflicts with the austere sexuality involved in the care of the self. Elaborating on Chapter Two's use of Foucault's (1978; 1984) *History of Sexuality*, modern sexual discourse has focused on austerity themes that have achieved a normalisation of heterosexual, monogamous, marital, in-the-flesh intercourse as natural, ethical, and morally justifiable. Within a larger philosophical view that understands sex as part of 'the care of the self', discourses of technique and pleasure have been replaced with discourses of morality and health (Foucault 1984). As evidenced by participants' responses in the previous chapter, erotic role-play, in its gameness and location in fantasy, invites a break from normative discourses of sexuality as it relates to both morality and health. Because of this break, erotic role-players have developed an alternate set of rules to define and describe which sexual acts are normative or naturalised for their purposes of play.

The first section of the chapter will look at data from the tabletop participants centred on how published rules are used to shape the inclusion of sexuality in their games. The section will begin by surveying officially published game guides and player handbooks the tabletop participants used in their gaming sessions for insight into the treatment of sexuality in the games they played. As part of the methodology, looking at game texts as they are used and referenced by participants provides insight into how both the fantasy genre and rules are interpreted by players and how published text functions during game play. The section will then move on to analyse focus-group data for insight into how official texts were interpreted and implemented by participants. The second section of this chapter will begin by discussing how erotic role-play is officially banned by *World of Warcraft*'s Terms of Use, and will then move on to discuss the tactical actions taken by players to continue to erotic role-play without getting caught. After Blizzard's official restrictions on ERP are established, the section will move on to discuss supplemental rules provided by the guild and individual participants of this study. This chapter will conclude by viewing how official rules and community-created rules governing erotic role-play are implemented to paradoxically invite play with sexual content and limit its effects.

TABLETOP RULES

The first role of published texts in the view of the participants of this study, both in terms of the games themselves as well as officially published background reading and lore, is to provide a basic environment, setting, and tone for game play. One of the first ways players familiarise them-selves with a game is through texts that establish setting and theme. Rather than create a completely new world to inhabit, settings and themes from role-playing texts were lifted from their sources and customised to fit the tabletop storyteller's vision of a campaign. Previous research has found this type of textual inspiration to be common among justifications to play. Many early role-playing games were heavily influenced by the rich detail of Tolkien's world in *The Lord of the Rings*, which players wanted to experience first hand (Dovey and Kennedy 2006; Barton 2008; Pearce and Artemesia 2009). Before the focus-group data on the role of rules can be discussed, it is important to explore the officially published rules and texts the tabletop group used in their role-play.

By using Fine's concept of diegesis (1983), published texts that outline the tone and setting for a role-play campaign can be considered a form of rules that provide a framework for incorporating sexuality into play. For example, the prologue of *Vampire: The Requiem* opens with interspersed stories written in different styles of white font set against a blood-red background depicting an abstract cityscape. These stories provide players with in-character accounts of life as a vampire as written by the game's developers. An example of such a story is reproduced below:

> Back to the booth, where dinner awaits. I can smell that she's excited, too, the dirty old whore, and you know what I mean by 'excited'.
> (From the prologue to *Vampire: The Requiem* by
> Marmell et al. 2004)

From reading the excerpt above and ones like it, players learn that not only is sexuality present in *Vampire* but also it is important enough to warrant inclusion in the prologue. Additionally, the way sexuality is presented reflects the mood, setting, and gives clues to the diegetic context of sex in the game. In the example above, players learn vampires can use erotic interaction to feed off unsuspecting humans. The way role-playing books contribute to players' treatment of erotic content through endogenous rules will be examined further.

There are several ludic mechanics in tabletop role-playing that outline how erotic actions can take place. In the tabletop group's favoured *World of Darkness* role-play system and setting, a 'seduction check'[1] is required if a player is trying to use their character's supernatural charm to gain false intimacy with another character. For vampires in particular, as the previous quote suggested, seducing other characters is an amusing way to hunt for blood. Rather than stalk and pounce, more socially inclined characters may find more enjoyment out of mentally manipulating mortals into surrendering themselves to be fed upon.

In *Vampire: The Masquerade* player's guide, seduction checks are subjected to both diegetic appropriateness and endogenous rules. As noted in Chapter Two, diegetic rules make reference to social or legal rules that affect characters in a game system and endogenous rules are the rules of the game itself that affect how the game is played (Björk and Holopainen

2003; Montola 2008). To elaborate, the player's handbook lists the four stages in a seduction, each requiring slightly different rolls of dice. The 'opening line', for example, requires a player to roll the number of ten-sided dice equal to their appearance and subterfuge scores (Rein-Hagen 1992, p. 217). The victim of this seduction is not entirely passive in this encounter, as the vampire-player must gain more successes than the victim's 'wits' score. The game master is allowed to boost the vampire's attempt by up to three points if they feel the opening line was particularly clever, and can likewise deduct successes from the player's roll if the line was particularly cheesy. Sometimes factors like the emotional state of the victim or inebriation will also contribute to additions or subtractions from the difficulty of the encounter.

The description of the highly quantified seduction check ends with a note about the diegetic appropriateness of involving such a mechanic in game play. The rule states, "If the emotions and motives are true, then you should ignore this system and role-play it out" (Rein-Hagen 1992, p. 217). I interpret this caveat as acknowledging both that legitimate seduction between characters may occur in the game system and legitimate seduction is more nuanced than a simple roll of dice. By stressing that if the emotions and motivations between the characters aren't falsified then the seduction check should be role-played out, the developer allows an erotic role-play to enter the game. This quote also shows awareness on the part of the developer about the tenuous interplay between the social (exogenous) rules and the game-defined (endogenous) rules during player interactions. Rules such as this one give players autonomy over their characters to decide if seduction between characters is a mechanical method of feeding, which can be resolved through a dice roll, or if it is part of the emotional or relationship developments of the character, which should be role-played. This rule is left intentionally open to interpretation so players and game masters may decide for themselves the appropriate depth and description of erotic content they want in their game.

If players want to limit the emotional or descriptive depth of erotic content in their games, they can choose to treat seduction as a dice roll and follow the rules outlined above. According to the participants, part of the joy, pleasure, and fun that comes from tabletop gaming emerges from situations like seduction checks. It is the mechanisation embraced by the undead in their attempt to imitate the living that causes some players to reflect upon affable patterns of human behaviour such as cheesy pick-up lines. Just as Henri Bergson wrote in his essay about comedy, "to imitate any one is to bring out the element of automatism he has allowed to creep into his person. ... This is the very essence of the ludicrous, it is no wonder that imitation gives rise to laughter" (1956, p. 12). Through the use of supernatural beings who have forgotten how to interact as human, the game makes light of mechanised human interaction in much the same way as Bergson's comedian. More than just making light of strained social actions, however, the game also uses vampires as a foil to reflect the supposed naturalness of human sexuality.

The multiphase process of attempting to seduce a victim reflects an over-complication of what is often presumed to be a fluid, natural, and pleasurable endeavour. In some ways, the rules and statistical determinations behind dice rolls for romantic social interactions help to peel back the socially ascribed layers of interaction and expose seduction as a social convention. As Foucault writes, the art of the self "underscores the need to subject that [sexual] activity to a universal form by which one is bound, a form grounded in both nature and reason, and valid for all human beings" (1984, p. 228). Rather than assume seduction for vampires is natural or reasonable, game rules point out it is often an overcomplicated social activity bound by physical appearance and ability to strategically lie to make oneself seem more desirable. As the last line of the description of seduction checks points out, however, if the emotions between characters are legitimate or arise out of a natural emotional development between characters, then special rules are no longer needed and the interaction can be role-played through players' unexamined, normative, and naturalised understanding of what legitimate seduction is.

The officially published rulebooks used by participants provided them with direction and context for sexuality in their games. By giving examples of how sexuality could be tied to a story, as in the opening excerpt, the game text opens itself for players and game masters to diegetically include erotic content in their games. The inclusion and detail of erotic mechanics, like seduction checks, are used by players to structure sexual practice within the game. The humorous treatment of many of these mechanics additionally provides critical insight into the presumed natural and normal state of human sexuality. Through looking at these few examples, it can be said that, within at least some game texts, details for how sexuality can be expressed are given. These details at once open the game to the inclusion of sexuality but also place limits on the types of sexuality that can be expressed. The seduction checks, for example, are only a valid mechanic so long as the erotic interest between characters is not genuine. By looking at the focus group responses from tabletop role-players, ideas about how these texts contribute to a discourse that limits sexual expression will be further developed.

FOCUS-GROUP DATA

Data from the tabletop focus group concentrates on how various game texts are interpreted by players. By seeing the practical employment of rules in game play, we gain a greater understanding of how published rules are used by players to create an alternate discourse of sexuality. As Foucault (1978) wrote, sexual discourse constitutes the ways in which sex and sexuality are spoken about and who does the speaking. Because players selectively relied on the games' textual rules to justify their inclusion of sexual content in their games, rules can be seen as contributing to a communally created discourse of erotic role-play. This section will use focus-group data to reference specific examples in which participants relied on endogenous, exogenous, and diegetic rules to influence their treatment of sexuality during game play. Utilising theory from Chapter Two, the participant responses will be read through the use of three types of rules: endogenous, exogenous, and diegetic. The role of rules in dictating the appropriateness of when, where, how, and to what effect sexual content is included in games will be further explored. Additionally, the argument will be made that players utilise rules to open themselves and their play to non-normative expressions and experiences of sexuality.

The focus group was designed to focus solely on sexual and erotic themes in role-play, so the participants' responses tended to focus on a few specific games in which sexuality was a key theme. Aside from the already mentioned *Dungeons and Dragons* and *Vampire: The Masquerade* games, *Werewolf: The Apocalypse* was a favourite among players. Werewolves are designed by the game's developers to rely on primal, violent, and sexual energy. This aspect of design was not lost on players, as participant Scott justified werewolves' overt sexuality by stating, "It's a rage thing, higher passions" in response to the focus-group question about mechanics. During the focus group, a follow-up question not in the original guide asked whether or not the respondents feel the sexual and sometimes violent themes they play with in-game reflect upon them as people. Their response, which harkens back to the *Werewolf: The Apocalypse* rulebook, emerged out of my thematic analysis of rules and is listed below:

> DAN: I'm ... not certain. To an extent, I'm playing in a playground they created and if they say this is what Black Spirals do, and I make a Black Spiral character which does that–
>
> SCOTT: It's following a lead.
>
> DAN: For example, a Black Spiral metis ahroun of high rank is going to be really fucking nasty. If the metis has fallen to the Wyrm, they will stop a fight to fuck a corpse of whatever they just killed. That is in the core *Werewolf* book.

Both Scott and Dan point to the published texts as justification for their character's design and behaviour, and indeed the justification is there. According to the core book they reference, the Black Spiral Dancers "are loathsome and evil, delighting in torture and pain" (Rein-Hagen et al. 1994, p. 46). From this excerpt we learn that if sex were to be included for Black Spiral Dancer players, it would only be included in a violent form of torture or pain. It would not be diegetically viable, for example, to play a Black Spiral Dancer who engaged with sex for the sake of tenderness or love.

In picking apart Dan's example character, the term 'metis' refers to the deformed offspring that results from two werewolves mating (Rein-Hagen et al. 1994). The Litany, or rather the in-game rules that govern werewolf society, dictates two weres must never mate. The deformed offspring is viewed as a curse, a bad omen, an aberration, or worse. The Black Spiral Dancers, who do not heed the Litany, have numerous metis in their ranks, which further stigmatises metis in other tribes. The term 'ahroun' refers to a set of abilities that define the character's role in a group; in other games this would be called the character's class. Ahroun are described as "the slayer, the mad man-wolf, Rage incarnate. Blood is his wine, war is his pleasure" (Rein-Hagen et al. 1994, p. 91). In researching the core text, we learn the type of werewolf Dan describes would be characterised by the game's authors as aggressive, fond of violence and pain, deformed, shunned, and entirely capable of committing unspeakable acts of violence and malice.

Because of the descriptions in *Werewolf's* player's guide, a Black Spiral metis ahroun character wishing to engage with sexual content would have several diegetic rules limiting the types of sexual behaviour available to them. However, the behaviour is limited in ways that subvert normalised concepts of appropriate sexual behaviour. As Foucault notes, moral systems are in place that "define other modalities of the relation to the self: a characterisation of the ethical substance based on finitude, the Fall, and evil; a mode of subjection in the form of obedience to a general law that is at the same time the will of a personal god; a type of work on oneself that implies a decipherment of the soul and a purificatory hermeneutics of the desires" (1984, p. 239). Read in this way, the Litany of werewolves represents the 'ethical substance' of modernity, which seeks to guide characters towards a purification of desires through obedience to general laws that may or may not represent the will of a religious figure. To role-play a character that does not heed the Litany is to therefore disregard the modern ethical and moral imperative that seeks to purify the self through restraint on sexual acts. By playing a character who 'will stop a fight to fuck a corpse', players are doing more than following a set of rules in a game, they are reshaping modern ethical substance to explore new possibilities beyond the constraints of humanist ethical practices. In using role-play settings and rules to restructure the performance of sexuality and gender in a way that questions ethics, morality, and even embraces evil, the participants are moving beyond the modern ethical substance in a way anticipated by Foucault. Dan comments the game's rules and text create a 'playground' for playing with such 'evil' concepts, which reflects an acknowledged separation from the primary social framework. Rather than address concerns over a perceived legitimation of such evil acts outside the game, the focus group makes clear such rules include subversive sexual content on a game level[2].

Aside from the diegetic rules placed on the acceptability of character behaviour, the rulebooks further provide endogenous rules for specific sexual acts. Just like the seduction check listed previously, these rules outline possible character abilities, actions, and enhancements. Just as Dan was justifying some of his characters' choices through their description in core books, he also discussed some of their more gruesome abilities as originating in various player guides. In the focus-group excerpt below, Joe questions an ability of a character Dan played, and Dan and Scott make reference to the book it is from.

> DAN [Looks at Scott]: I'm just playing according to the book!
> JOE: The fourteen-inch barbed penis–
> DAN: Is a power from *Freak Legion*.
> SCOTT [Looks at the Interviewer and Nods]: It is, actually.

After Dan reasserts he is playing with the texts the publishers have given him, Joe interrupts and questions Dan with one of the most extreme abilities employed in Dan's role-playing past. *Freak Legion*, a book published by Black Dog, the World of Darkness gaming system's adult publisher, does indeed list fourteen-inch barbed penises as a special power called Savage Genitalia. The description in the book reads: "the fomor (regardless of gender) has genitals with some menacing feature. Male variations include excessive length (14"+) or hardness, thorns, sandpaper texture or curved barbs" (Bridges 1995, p. 37). Through this example, the influence rulebooks have on play can clearly be seen. Dan suggests he develops characters with grotesque sexual abilities and violent sexual behaviours because the games' rulebooks detail it as befitting for certain types of characters. Dan's reliance on game texts to justify his inclusion of extreme sexual acts in game play illuminates the power of officially published rules in the player-created discourse of acceptable acts.

Borrowing a concept from Roger Caillois' (1961) description of play in Chapter Two, the particular texts Dan references aid him in an exploration of the mysterious. The mysterious, in this case, is the extreme emotional discomfort associated with coerced and violent sex. The unfortunate and damaging experience of rape is one Dan and the tabletop group would never want to experience first hand but could explore with relative safety in a play environment. Aside from curiosity, the benefit of playing with such a dark and emotionally difficult theme comes from the extreme emotional response it conjures in the players. Other researchers studying similar fields of extreme sexual role-play have pointed out there are myriad complex, emotional meanings involved in such play (Montola 2010; Harviainen 2012). An example is needed in order to fully realise how the endogenous rules, including ones that outline possible sexual abilities, are employed by Dan to explore the darker mysteries of sexual violence. He continued this section of the focus group by describing his favourite erotic role-play session, which involved the character with the fourteen-inch barbed penis.

DAN: [The other characters] had managed to drag [his character's lover] off and throw him into Malfius, which is sort of the waste-disposal shoot for good werewolves. So he came back as a rank two Spiral Ahroun. First thing he did was hunt down [Dan's character] in his little cave where he would play music, bugger him senseless, and then run off into the night. At which point, [Dan's character] ended up committing suicide. He was one of my favourite characters. The party was still going, it just seemed this character had reached the point of no return. Yeah, and that was played out all on camera.

INTERVIEWER: Why was it your favourite?

DAN: Um, because it was basically the perfect kind of character development.

SCOTT [Nods Sympathetically]: It played to a natural end.

DAN: It pretty much nailed the *World of Darkness* to a T, you know, it doesn't matter how nice you are, it doesn't matter if you have true love, if you have hope or the rest of it, chances are you are going to die horribly. The end. I just feel like it was the perfect simulation of the game system, really. Pretty much one of my favourite characters ever ended up killing himself before the campaign's end and I still think it was worthwhile.

In Dan's retelling of his experience, we see how playing with difficult and dark themes can be emotionally troubling but also rewarding. Through the group's role-play, a powerful narrative of love had emerged between two characters. The theme, setting, and rules based on how certain types of characters should behave caused the true love between Dan's character and his lover to dramatically change. As events unfolded in the storytelling aspect of the game, and characters developed and changed due to their environments, diegetic and endogenous rules were used to exploit players' emotional attachments to their characters for the sake of exploring the mystery of grief, bereavement, and loss. Evidence for this is most easily seen in the way Dan describes the session as his favourite.

Dan justifies his enjoyment of this scene by placing emphasis on how well the character fit within the diegetic rules in terms of the characters' behaviour and how this contributed towards an emotionally charged narrative. When Dan reflects on the events that had led to his character's death, he does so within the frame of the character's available knowledge and experience. Although as a player he could have made the choice to not end the life of his character, he did so anyway because within the context of the narrative, this was not his choice to make. As Scott offers, Dan's character's life 'played to a natural end'. Recognising he had lost his true love, both character and player realised the character had 'reached the point of no return' and could not, in accordance with the events of the story, be redeemed. On the level of the player, Dan comments on how well this campaign fit within the overarching, diegetic rules on themes and settings of *The World of Darkness* as a whole. Part of Dan's enjoyment from this campaign stems from how it marries with his conception of how a *World of Darkness* role-playing game should be run.

In Dan's comments on the worthwhileness of the campaign, despite his loss of a favourite character, we are afforded a glimpse into the powerful emotional impact of sexuality in role-play games. It is not a difficult argument to make to say most people would never want to experience the emotional trauma of losing a loved one in such a way as Dan's character. However, when the mystery of such an experience is juxtaposed in a playful environment with no permanent repercussions, players like Dan find such a prospect appealing. Playing with difficult concepts often results in a memorable experience. As noted in Chapter Three, research into extreme live-action role-play (LARP) communities has emerged with similar findings. When studying a LARP entitled *Gang Rape*, in which participants take turns playing the roles of victim and rapist, Markus Montola (2010) found players enjoyed such extreme games because of the intense feelings and emotions they provoked.

Playing with difficult, sensitive, and emotionally charged concepts and themes, even with rulebook justification, requires a level of diegetic involvement on the part of the players. An unspoken, but implicitly understood, exogenous rule for the tabletop respondents was that every character action should have diegetic justification. Dan, speaking as the group's lead storyteller and dungeon master, described a time in which he felt uncomfortable moderating a game when a player tried to insert a violent rape into a storyline where he felt it was unwarranted.

> DAN: Um, a player did try to drop in what appeared to be a completely gratuitous rape scene for no apparent reason.
> INTERVIEWER: Oh. And did you stop them, or–
> DAN [Makes a Slapping Motion WITH HIS HAND]: Bad player. No biscuit.
> JOE: Whereas if you were playing *Forgotten Realms* ... um ... uhh. Feru, is it? The Goddess of Exquisite Pain?
> DAN: Scahrossar?
> JOE: Yeah, that would make perfect sense.
> DAN: Yes, but he wasn't. I don't quite know where it came from.
> SCOTT: As he said, it was completely uncalled for in the situation.
> DAN: Yeah, if the situation warrants it, which is entirely up to the capricious whims of me, the DM [dungeon master], then I'll allow it. It's not that I even have any particular problem with it, it's just it needs to have a point and a purpose. In the same way I wouldn't expect a party to stop to break dance.

As Dan reflects on the situation and his response to it, he points out he is not objecting to the use of rape in a game in which sexual violence is allowed by the rules but only when it seems at odds with the narrative. This perhaps reflects his, and many others', attitude that some types of extreme content make role-play memorable and a valuable experience (Montola 2010). Dan describes how the player's insistence on including this scene made him uncomfortable because he felt as though the player was seeking to use the scene to fulfil an out-of-character sexual desire. Here a crucial split in values is made between intense role-play for the sake of role-play versus for the sake of sexual gratification. Going back to the previous discussion in which Dan retold his favourite role-play session of all time, we are again confronted with the importance of boundary management. In order for uncomfortable topics to be explored, they must remain in the diegetic and be discussed afterward within the frame of player and not the primary social frame. Dan effectively used the exogenous rule he and the role-playing group had created: that player actions must have a diegetic justification to prevent an uncomfortable, gratuitous rape scene from entering game play. This example additionally shows how rules are carefully read and employed by participants to create a discourse of acceptability that is selective in its application.

Revisiting the importance of officially published texts in setting boundaries for the appropriateness of sexual content in role-playing, Joe attempts to think of a scenario in which a rape scene would be appropriate. Scahrossar, as mentioned by Joe, is a Goddess discussed in the *Book of Vile Darkness*, a supplementary *Dungeons and Dragons* guide intended for use in evil campaign settings. In the book, she is described as a "woman covered entirely in tight, studded black leather so that even her face is concealed. ... [Her temples] are hidden behind false facades. ... [And her] rooms are soundproofed to muffle the cries of pain. ... Altars are usually baroque monstrosities of spikes, spines, clamps, and chains" (Cook et al. 2002, pp. 11–12). Joe's and Dan's readily accessible and accurate knowledge of Scahrossar demonstrates their reliance on published game texts to provide context for the inclusion of erotic content in game play.

In studying excerpts from role-playing texts and the responses from the tabletop role-playing group, several important themes have emerged that elaborate on how rules function to shape the inclusion of sexuality into role-play. Most notable is the idea that rulebooks simultaneously provide justification for including sexuality in role-playing games and place limitations on which types of sexual expression are acceptable. This helps to answer the primary research question by showing rules in some ways provide a gateway for non-normative sexuality to enter play.

By establishing key narrative topics, role-playing handbooks provide players with textual recourse should their decision to include erotic themes in role-play be questioned. Dan's reliance on *Werewolf: The Apocalypse*'s description of Black Spiral Dancer behaviour to justify his play with rape gives insight into how game texts provide an entry point for non-normative, amoral, and violent sexual themes to enter play. Rather than indiscriminately playing with potentially harmful concepts, however, the same books provide contextualisation and limitation for such behaviour. In Dan's retelling of his favourite erotic role-play session, the mysterious emotional trauma of rape, bereavement, and loss was explored in a structured play environment. The extreme and potentially harmful emotions invoked by the play session were managed through the use of rules, which helped ensure the diegetic and primary social frames remained separate.

The importance of maintaining an environment in which narrative cohesion was kept to a high standard was reflected in Dan's management of a player who wanted to include a gratuitous rape scene for an unjustified reason. In enforcing the exogenous house rules and reflecting on certain endogenous rules that would render such acts as appropriate, Joe and Dan once again stressed the importance of keeping erotic role-play within the diegetic for the purposes of a cohesive and meaningful story. Keeping these themes in mind, the next section will discuss the responses from the *World of Wacraft* participants.

WORLD OF WARCRAFT'S RULES

This section will explore the use of rules by the *World of Warcraft* participants to shape and structure erotic role-play. Through this exploration, insight will be given into how players use rules to both allow for erotic content to be experienced in play and also restrict the types of sexuality expressed and where they can be expressed. The primary research question will be answered by reflecting on how the various types of rules encountered and used by the *World of Warcraft* participants influence the ability to freely play with sexuality in the game.

There are many similarities between the *World of Warcraft* and tabletop responses involving rules but there are importantly many differences. *World of Warcraft*'s visual format and its online nature make the game's rules regarding erotic role-play stringently prohibitive when compared to tabletop games. Perhaps due to cultural conventions that place age requirements on the viewing of pornography but not the reading of textual erotica, and the lack of practical and reliable means to verify age, *World of Warcraft* has rules to exclude sexual language and text from the game, whereas many tabletop games have included rules to encourage it. The Terms of Use (ToU) provides exogenous rules that attempt to filter content in the game from outside by regulating player communication. Rather than altogether expunging erotic role-play from the game, however, players have adapted their ERP to accommodate Blizzard's restrictions using resources provided by the game itself. The erotic role-players in this study adapted their community's and their personal standards of play to include endogenous and diegetic rules that are designed to protect themselves both from players who would seek to abuse the sexual freedoms of the online format and from being banned from the game.

This section begins by looking at the officially published rules put forth by Blizzard, which define erotic role-play as an offense requiring disciplinary action. These rules are then compared to the rules developed by the guild, which seek to protect its members' privacy and prevent them from getting caught. Finally, the section ends by reviewing the rules developed by individual players to ensure their erotic role-play sessions are safe and consensual. Overall, all three types of rules are read as formulating a type of discourse that defines available language, setting, and location for the expression of sexuality under rigid terminology.

WORLD OF WARCRAFT'S OFFICIAL RULES

Unlike the rulebooks mentioned by the tabletop group, which helpfully provided context for times when sexual themes might be included in play, the official rules found in *World of Warcraft*'s ToU seek to ban sexual content from the game altogether. Erotic role-play itself is not explicitly banned or even named. The only section of the original ToU that has been cited by Blizzard game masters as applying to erotic role-play comes from the guidelines for chat because most erotic role-play takes place through the use of the game's chat function. These guidelines are reproduced below:

> When engaging in Chat, you may not:
> (i) Transmit or post any content or language which, in the sole and absolute discretion of Blizzard, is deemed to be offensive, including without limitation content or language that is unlawful, harmful, threatening, abusive, harassing, defamatory, vulgar, obscene, hateful, sexually explicit, or racially, ethnically or otherwise objectionable, nor may you use a misspelling or an alternative spelling to circumvent the content and language restrictions listed above. ...
> (vi) Harass, threaten, stalk, embarrass or cause distress, unwanted attention or discomfort to any user of the Game.
>
> (Blizzard Entertainment 2004)

From the list of prohibited chat topics, 'sexually explicit' language and language that causes 'discomfort' for other players are the only circumstances under which consensual erotic role-play could be considered against the rules. Nevertheless, these rules that define what cannot be discussed in chat help to develop a discourse of sexuality in the game. As Foucault reminds us, "silence itself – the things one declines to say, or is forbidden to name, the discretion that is required between different speakers – is less the absolute limit of discourse ... than an element that functions alongside the things said" (1978, p. 27). Through banning sexually explicit language, Blizzard has contributed to a discourse of sexuality in *World of Warcraft* that obliges erotic role-players to be mindful that conventional linguistic manifestations of sex are actively prohibited within some parts of the game's architecture. In response, erotic role-players have developed tactics that evade Blizzard's imposed silence. The rules found in the Terms of Use are viewed alongside erotic role-players' tactical evasion through the modification of performance and practices as a defining feature of the experience of erotic role-play.

Blizzard eventually revisited the chat rules listed above and expanded on its definitions of offensive behaviour after the game faced negative media attention. Similar to the moral panic involving accusations of paedophiles operating in videogame arcades in the early 1980s (Williams 2006), gaming media outlets reported stories about an 'extreme' erotic role-play guild in *World of Warcraft* that supported paedophilia as part of their in-game erotic role-play (Watchowski 2007). Blizzard responded by disbanding the offending guild and by tightening their ToU policies involving general sexual themes. In an article referenced by game masters on Battle.net, a network of sites for Blizzard's games and products, inappropriate chat is defined as being "crude and offensive in nature … an inappropriate reference to human anatomy or bodily functions … pornographic in nature" (Blizzard Entertainment 2010). This elaboration further contributes towards a discourse of stigmatisation as the terms 'crude', 'offensive', and 'inappropriate' are applied to any sexual themes in game chat. This now infamous example, and Blizzard's response to it, was cited by participants in this study as a cautionary reminder of how careful they need to be not only to verify the age of their partners but also to be discrete about their in-game erotic role-play.

To date, Blizzard has never given a reason for its stance on inappropriate chat other than pointing to and redefining their Terms of Use. Many players[3] have speculated on the role of the Entertainment Software Review Board's (ESRB) ratings and possible influences on Blizzard's policies. In the United States, the game has a Teen rating by the ESRB. The ratings given to games by the ESRB are intended to function, like film rating certificates, as a guide for concerned parents who wish to control the media their children consume. A rating of Teen indicates "content that may be suitable for ages 13 and older [that] … may contain violence, suggestive themes, crude humor, minimal blood, simulated gambling, and/or infrequent use of strong language" (ESRB 2012). The only category under which erotic role-play might appear are the 'suggestive themes', which the ESRB defines as "mild provocative references or materials" (ESRB 2012).

There does, however, seem to be a set precedent within online gaming and the fantasy genre that prohibits or limits sexual content. Recalling from Chapter Three, past research into a different MMORPG found Sony Entertainment, publishers of *Everquest*, ordered creators of erotic fan fiction featuring characters from the game to remove the stories they had published on forums and websites (Taylor 2006). Sony felt the erotic content was at odds with the 'family friendly' image of the game they wished to portray (Taylor 2006). It would appear as though both Sony and Blizzard are concerned with not only keeping a 'family friendly' public reputation to avoid censure but also make efforts to avoid unwanted attention from media regulatory bodies and the law.

Functionally, the enforcement of these rules has dictated where and how ERP can take place in the game. Through fear of an account ban, erotic role-players will not publically ERP or discuss ERP and have instead found private alternatives. In order to discuss the alternative methods used by erotic role-players, it is first worth outlining how disciplinary action works in the game. The previously discussed behavioural guidelines are enforceable through the game itself via a function available in the players' interface. Players are able to police each other's behaviour by contacting a game master to file a complaint about offensive behaviour. After the complaint is submitted, a game master reviews the case and decides on appropriate disciplinary action. The actions taken by game masters range from a warning e-mail to an account ban. It is this fear that has made erotic role-players explore alternative, private methods of communicating in and out of the game.

It is the responsibility of offended players to report others for unacceptable behaviour. Although this type of peer-reporting is still the primary method of policing in-game behaviour, additional methods have been employed due to pressure from the press. In the late summer of 2010, Blizzard announced for the first time that game masters would patrol known problem areas specifically to apprehend erotic role-players (McCurley 2010). These areas are well known by players and game masters alike, and have often been the topic of fan-created videos and songs. An example of such a song is below:

> *Goldshire's ERPing, Yiffin' druid furries, Hope your inn burns down.*
> *From 'End of the World (of Warcraft)', parody music video by phrog801*
> *(2010)*[4]

Similar to the bars and clubs of the real world, there are certain areas in the game in which erotic role-play is easy to find. The lyrics above, for example, come from a YouTube video that parodies the popular song 'End of the World as We Know It (And I Feel Fine)' by REM. The fan-created video was released just before the Cataclysm expansion on November 7, 2010 and features coverage of the geographical changes in the game. Because of Blizzard's promise to patrol Goldshire's[5] Inn for erotic role-play, fans speculated the area might be removed from the game altogether under the guise of a dragon attack to prevent future problems.

Goldshire is known in the game as a red-light district of sorts. The Inn functions both as a social space where characters can negotiate romantic and erotic interactions, like a bar or nightclub, and a space rife with prostitution. Much like red-light districts in the real world, places like Goldshire cause controversy amongst the citizens of *World of Warcraft*. Players often have split opinions on the existence of such locations. Reader responses to an article from a *World of Warcraft* webzine that detailed Blizzard's plan to patrol Goldshire ranged from outrage and disgust at the types of activities rumoured to take place there to humour and finally to echoes of practicality (McCurley 2010). One prevailing opinion[6] is that if a location known for ERP is shut down or heavily patrolled, the activity will simply move somewhere else.

By comparing the official rules from *World of Warcraft* listed in this section to the official rules published in books used by the tabletop group, some comparisons can be made that help illuminate how rules function to structure erotic content in games and answer the secondary research questions. Firstly, rather than creating rules that support the inclusion of sexual themes in games, the behavioural guidelines listed in *World of Warcraft*'s Terms of Use attempt to ban them from entering game play. From this attempt, a discourse that defines sexual content as forbidden shapes how erotic role-play happens. Rather than succeeding in expunging sexual content in play, the chat rules merely refine how it is included. Players know, for example, to avoid areas such as Goldshire where game masters reportedly patrol. Additionally, instead of using the commands / emote and /say, which would make the descriptions of their actions and conversations publicly available to anyone nearby, players use whispers and party-chat functions to selectively limit who can view their text[7]. Both the whisper and party-chat functions are parts of the official game code and were originally designed to facilitate player communication in reaching the game's objectives.

Player's reappropriation of chat channels reflects a technological difference in the mesh of ludic and diegetic rules between tabletop and *WoW* participants. Whereas tabletop participants could discuss the rules found in game guides with the game master and collectively negotiate the amount and content of erotic role-play in their game, *WoW* game masters are faceless entities only invoked when rules need to be enforced. As detailed through the description of players' self-policing through the report function above, game masters are only called on to resolve conflicts between players and the rules. Whilst game masters are most often called on to solve glitches and bugs within the game that prevent players from completing objectives, as in a literal conflict between the player-character and the encoded rules that define the game's environment and functionality, they also handle disputes concerning the exogenous social rules. As there are no endogenous rules that allow characters to mimic sexual acts through their avatars, meaning there are no endogenous rules/codes within the game that allow sexual acts to be animated, game masters receiving complaints about erotic role-play are only concerned with potential breaches of the game's Terms of Use. Once a game master has reviewed chatlogs and determined whether a ToU rule was broken, there is little conversation between them and the offending party other than a formal notice of what disciplinary action, if any, will be issued. So while official rules for the tabletop group allowed for erotic role-play both endogenously, through providing ludic mechanics for erotic actions, and exogenously, through conversations with the game master about the appropriateness of various acts, *World of Warcraft*'s technology and Terms of Use offer neither. Ultimately, the inflexibility of *WoW*'s computer-mediated rules affected erotic role-play in practice by giving players the impetus to manipulate the technology provided and find ways around the Terms of Use through private chat channels, out-of-game communication, reappropriating in-game items through descriptive text, and self-created artwork and stories. The official rules' lack of support for erotic actions additionally gave players impetus to create their own rules, which will be discussed below.

WORLD OF WARCRAFT AND GUILD RULES

Guild rules, or house rules, which may otherwise be referred to as exogenous rules (Björk and Holopainen 2003; Montola 2008), refer to community-created rules not embedded in official game texts but emerging from social-play experiences. Although many of these rules are implied in most games, such as no speaking out-of-character during in-character scenes, the *World of Warcraft* participants elaborated on rules specifically concerning erotic role-play. These rules are viewed as a type of discourse and this section concerns how participants created and implemented these guild rules and the effect their implementation had on erotic role-play.

The participants, having the technology available to them, listed their specific rules on the guild's age-restricted forum. This area of the forum requires viewers to be members of the guild, so common web surfers are unable to view its content, and be over the age of eighteen. Although the legal age of consent varies by country and even by state, eighteen was specifically chosen by the guild as it is the age required in North America to purchase or view sexually explicit content. The guild leader informed me this rule was set in place to avoid accusations of paedophilia. It is required that any member wishing to participate in erotic role-play read, understand, and practice the rules listed on the forum. Failure to do so results in punishment ranging from a chat with officers to the temporary removal of certain privileges to removal from the guild. The first post that readers of the adult forum are greeted by was authored by the guild leaders with input from trusted officers and contains the four specific rules listed here:

1 Try to keep OOC down. It's perfectly fine to ((bracket speak)) in a large open thread if you need to work something out, but try to keep most OOC chatter to PMs [private messages].
2 Do not, under any circumstances, tag people for adult RP without asking them first. I know this is mentioned above but it is – especially – the case here. That's creepy and rude.

3 In addition to tagging whether your post is Open or Closed, please tag in the very first line of the first post what will be taking place in this thread, such as sex (Het, Homo, BDSM), violence (death, torture, rape), whatever (Re-enacting every single George Carlin skit).
4 Absolutely No Paedophilic RP, at all, ever. I don't care if the child character is being played by someone 18+ all individuals in this forum must be 18+, mentally and physically.

The first rule asks that all out-of-character discussions are talked about elsewhere. Its place as the first guild rule is significant in that it stresses the importance of maintaining immersion in the fantasy of role-play. Immersion is a popular concept in the field of game-studies literature and has been defined as a "metaphorical term derived from the physical experience of being submerged in water ... the sensation of being surrounded by a completely other reality, as different as water is from air, that takes over all of our attention, our whole perceptual apparatus" (Murray 1997, pp. 98–99). The effect of a rule that attempts to secure immersion is twofold. At once it demands that players "create a character who transcends the mechanic of the game and takes on a plausible, defined reality of its own" (MacCallum-Stewart and Parsler 2008, p.226) while still keeping the character within the themes and stylistic elements of the game.

Similar to when Dan disciplined a player who gratuitously tried to insert a rape scene into game play, the first rule stresses that characters and their erotic stories should be able to function on their own in the lore of the game without out-of-character support. The character must remain digetically real, which is to say their story must be plausible within the setting and themes of *World of Warcraft*. Without this reference back to the game, the character loses its cohesion and the narrative, which makes it role-play and differentiates it from cybersex. This first rule also requires the player to focus not only on the larger body of fiction created by the games' developer but also on the narrative they create with another player. Previous research into role-playing in *World of Warcraft* has found that while fiction describes an imaginary world, narratives specifically tell of the events that take place there (Klastrup 2008), and it is in these narratives that the most meaningful player interactions take place.

The second rule states that 'tagging,' or mentioning, another player's character in an erotic post or a story without their consent is both 'creepy' and 'rude'. On the surface, the effect of this rule has little to do with the game's mechanics or fiction and concerns the social behaviour of players outside the game. It functions in much the same way as various social norms do in the out-of-game world (Mortensen 2008). Just as a person who brags about their sexual exploits may be reminded not to kiss and tell, so too are erotic role-players and their characters cautioned against talking about their sexual activities, be they actual or fantasised.

The effect of this rule is twofold. At once players are reminded to respect each other's privacy concerning intimate issues for the sake of being polite and for the sake of avoiding bans from the game. As detailed earlier in this section, Blizzard's policing of public erotic role-play is a concern for erotic role-players. In order to ensure the guild and its members are not caught participating in an activity against the ToU, a rule such as this one needs to emphasise the importance of discretion. Adding credence to the claim that this rule was adopted in reaction to Blizzard's policies on sexual content, there is no equivalent in the tabletop group's rulebooks or house rules.

The third rule, as listed in the forum, asks that the author titles the post with keywords so readers are not shocked or distressed by what they find. More than a rule exclusive to online experiences, the idea of warning readers and players about the themes that will be featured in a game seems to be an act of courtesy. One of the rulebooks used by the tabletop group, for example, includes a reader advisory in the introduction that states, "It is only fair to warn you that this book is gross" (Bridges 1995, p. 13). Likewise, during the focus group, Dan detailed warning players of potential themes before they start a campaign. In both cases, openly advertising potential themes to be covered helps define acceptable and unacceptable sexual themes for role-play.

For the *World of Warcraft* players, this rule additionally targets people who find fun and humour in causing conflict and turmoil over posts with extreme and offensive content. These players are termed in contemporary Internet vernacular as "trolls", but they have been discussed in other terms as well. Brian Sutton-Smith (2001, p. 150) writes about spoilsports as "being ruled by some other rules of play. The rest of us know he won't play by the usual rules of decorum or according to the usual meanings of words, but he will in general stay metaphorically 'on stage' when he shocks us with his fantasies". The troll exists to expose the fantasy espoused by player narratives as a farce and does so in an extreme, shocking, and sometimes humorous ways. By posting the rules prominently as the first entry in the adult forums, the guild is able to establish infrastructure and create consequences for actions that would hurt players or the guild by demeaning and devaluing the erotic role-play experience.

The final rule states that paedophilic role-play is disallowed under any circumstance. The inclusion of this very specific rule conflates normative ideas of sexual taboo. If paedophilia is specifically disallowed but other taboos go unmentioned, then are the guild's feelings on bestiality or necrophilia negotiable? When questioned about this rule in particular, several guild members pointed to the previously mentioned disbanding of a guild that featured paedophilic content (Wachowski 2007). Because this was the first publicised instance of Blizzard stopping erotic role-play, as opposed to simply ignoring it, communities of players took notice and sought to prevent a similar measure taken against them.

Looking at the guild-created rules on erotic role-play has answered the primary research question by showing the ways players attempt to include and regulate sexual behaviour when official sources refuse to. Rather than providing guidelines for acceptable sexual content in the game, Blizzard's outright ban led the guild to create rules to protect themselves from intrusions of privacy and a potential ban. Likewise, certain rules were included as exogenous house rules to help keep erotic content focused on diegetic character interactions. This focus is central in separating erotic role-play from cybersex[8]. Furthermore, separating the two contributes to a discourse about what erotic content in games is, or rather what it should be. In continuing the discussion of rules as discourse that serves to manage the boundaries of play and the exploration of sexual mysteries, the next section explores individual player rules.

WORLD OF WARCRAFT AND INDIVIDUAL RULES

In order to express gender and sexuality, participants of this study seemed to appreciate the reassurance that rules provide. The guild's rules provide players with a focus on in-character coherence, privacy, and disclosure. These rules were respected by all guild members during the time of fieldwork, with no incident requiring disciplinary action. The guild seemed successful in establishing a safe space for its members to explore the mysteries of gender and sexuality through play. However, not all members of the *World of Warcraft* guild erotic role-play solely with other members. For erotic role-play with members outside the guild, a few participants created individual exogenous rules.

Without the screening process used by the guild and its forum, players needed to create their own rules and enforce personal boundaries during erotic role-play sessions. An example of this comes from an interview with participant Greenhat. During her interview she discusses and explains the house rules she has created for her erotic role-play sessions.

> GREENHAT (GH): I want to note that there are some ERP kind of rules that I have that may be interesting.
> INTERVIEWER: Rules?
> GH: Yeah rules. You know how you're in a dungeon and everyone knows to need on stuff only if they need it[9], but if they need on everything everyone assumes they are ninjas? Kinda like that it's hard to explain … It's the … non-stated non-verbal rules … but you do it to be polite.
> INTERVIEWER: Like rules of consent?
> GH: Nah … it's more like … no one-handed typing. Save it for after XD, or try to put as many details into the ERP as the other person

> is doing. It's always rude to be in the middle of a session ... just
> sitting there and wait 20 minutes or I've even had the person sign
> off in the middle and have the person come back and be like ...
> "Oh man that was great I just jacked off. ..." That's rude.

In order to explain the social nature of her rules, Greenhat compares them to more generic social rules concerning the division of gear at the end of a boss fight or dungeon. After many players have worked together to kill a difficult enemy, the enemy's possessions are taken as a reward. The division of these possessions and deciding who gets what is often an area of contention for groups. Some players have sought to avoid the contention by sneakily stealing the prizes and disappearing, like a ninja. Greenhat's comparison between 'ninja-looting', as the process is called, and 'one-handed' typing points out the similarities between two exogenous rules that try to enforce a social code of honour within the larger context of endogenous rules.

In addition to showing just how rule-bound erotic role-play is, Greenhat offers insight into how the spoilsport, or troll, might enter into an erotic role-play scenario. For Greenhat, ERP is as much a chance to show off writing skills as it is an opportunity to become physically aroused. This collaborative storytelling requires voluntary participation by all parties involved for the goals to be met, in this case the development of a backstory, character motivations, or an alternate plotline. Rather than co-operatively telling a story or contributing to the overall narrative of the characters, the spoilsport plays along only so far as necessary for their own needs to be met.

Although the one-handed typer may begin the erotic role-play session by expressing a sincere interest in sharing a narrative with another character, this is but part of their own game, which is to maintain the façade of genuine interest until their arousal and climax are met. Once climax occurs, the spoilsport has won their game and will stop playing, leaving the other player or players without closure or climax. The spoilsport leaves other players to ascribe what meaning, if any, the encounter had on their character's narrative. The diegetic meaning, if there ever were one, is lost. Because of her experiences with one-handed typers, Greenhat went on to mention that she now employs preventative measures to avoid these players. She now conducts a brief, trial ERP session in which she determines whether or not the player is worthy of booking in for a full two-hour slot.

While Greenhat developed her rules to protect her from spoilsports, another player developed rules to help maintain the bleed between player and character. Referring back to the first guild rule, which asks that players try to keep out-of-character chatter to a minimum, Penpy developed a similar rule for himself by limiting his contact with the players of his ERP partners. This rule developed after a difficult conversation with his wife wherein Penpy realised he was having difficulty keeping his erotic role-play in the game.

INTERVIEWER: How did you go about discussing ERP with [your wife]?

PENPY: It wasn't easy. I wasn't open about it at first. She knew that I RPed, but there was an issue when I allowed things at the beginning of my RP 'career' on *WoW* when things bled over into OOC with another player. Luckily, I was able to collar that and never allow it to happen again. I decided I needed to be honest with my wife about how I spent my time in the game, and explained to her that my characters had relationships and that sometimes that meant that there were erotic themes taking place.

INTERVIEWER: If it's not too personal, how did you manage the 'bleeding'? Or, if that question is a bit much, how do you ensure things stay in-character now?

PENPY: Well it's much like in real life. Things started innocently enough with private OOC conversation with a flirtation here and there, then escalated quickly to more. I had to cut off contact with that person completely to make sure that the problem was stamped out. Now, I am just very careful with how far I let my flirtatious nature go.

Penpy's decision to 'collar' his flirtatious nature and keep out-of-character contact to a minimum reflects several of the themes in this chapter. First, while non-normative sexual themes may be played with in the game, the rule of limiting erotic content to characters prevents it from crossing over into players' lives. This brings forth the role of the diegetic in shaping erotic role-play. Similarly, this creates important connections to Foucault's idea of the regulatory faculties of austere sexuality. In order to morally, ethically, and medically purify oneself, sexuality and its connections to evil and disease must be carefully managed (Foucault 1984). Speaking about the institution of marriage in particular, Foucault writes that marriage under the modifications of sexual austerity and the care of the self "mainly concerns the valorisation of the conjugal bond and the dual relation that constitutes it; the husband's right conduct and the moderation he needs to enjoin on himself are not justified merely by considerations of status, but by the nature of the relationship, its universal form and the mutual obligations that derive from it" (1984, p. 238). There is a moral and ethical imperative for marriage to be monogamous, and as Foucault notes, this imperative may take the physical form of a 'conjugal bond' that stands as a physical manifestation of 'mutual obligations' enacted in a marital relationship. Therefore in order to conform to cultural mandates that emphasise the bonds of marriage as being dualistically exclusive, Penpy needed to collar his 'flirtatious nature'. Here, Penpy can be seen as subject to multiple sexual economies. There is, on the one hand, the economy present in in his primary social frame that dictates the conjugal bond of marriage should be monogamous, and on the other the economy present in erotic role-play that fosters, if not encourages, sexual exploration. In order to manage both, he creates a type of personal rule that places limits on how far he lets his flirtatious nature go. Such a rule additionally harkens back to the first guild rule, which also attempts to separate the sexual economies of the primary social frame and the diegetic frame by asking erotic role-players keep out-of-character talk to a minimum.

By looking at these two interview responses, the ability of players' own rules to influence what is and is not included in erotic play is seen. This helps to answer the primary research question by showing how boundaries for the inclusion of sexual content are managed at an individual level. Importantly, in comparison to the tabletop group, these responses show how a lack of official rules supporting the inclusion of sexual content leads players to create their own in an effort to manage, in Foucault's terms, their care of the self. In order to limit the sexual mysteries being explored, Greenhat and Penpy both created and employed rules to limit their experiences to the diegetic realm and, in Penpy's case, to manage the multiple sexual economies he is subjected to when erotic role-playing. In doing so, they have illustrated the steps taken to ensure erotic role-play remains a safe space to experience themes vicariously through characters by showing the discomfort caused when ERP moves out-of-character and into the primary social frame. For Greenhat, this happened when players would pause a session to masturbate and for Penpy, this happened when he began extramaritally flirting with another player. Both cases illustrate how erotic role-play at once invites socially constrained or otherwise amoral sexual activities to be played with and also limits the extent to which the experiences gained in erotic play can hold subversive meaning outside the context of the game.

CONCLUSION

This chapter answered the primary research question by showing how rules paradoxically open up and limit erotic role-play for the exploration of non-normative sexuality. For the tabletop group, this was achieved through knowledge and use of the officially published game texts. The game texts themselves provide functional mechanics for the incorporation of sexual abilities, as in the examples of seduction checks and the character ability Savage Genitalia. During the focus group, the participants discussed how specific breeds of werewolves had specific sexual personalities attributed to them. Both Dan and Scott recalled how for Black Spiral Dancers, sex is a violent and painful experience while Joe gave an example of how a lengthy rape scene could be appropriate in a tabletop campaign through his knowledge of the goddess Scahrossar. In the first example, werewolves and the use of the Litany in the tabletop game were analysed as providing a moral system or, in Dan's words, a 'playground' in which 'evil' sexual acts could be played with. Dan's response showed how players open sexuality for a type of play that questions ethics, morality, and even embraces evil within the game's safe distance from the ethical substance of the primary social framework. Joe's example of Scahrossar was analysed as indicative of the group's extensive knowledge and easy application of the games' texts. This, in turn, answered the secondary research questions by emphasising the importance of official text in providing precedent for sexual content to enter the games.

Unlike the tabletop group's wealth of texts and rules concerning the exogenic appropriateness, endogenic function, and diegetic theme of sexual content, the *World of Warcraft* participants were given only prohibiting rules stating sexual content of any kind is banned from the game. The game's Terms of Use, which now bans explicit sexual language specifically, was the primary source of official rules banning ERP referenced by players and game masters alike. From observational notes, discussions with players, and past research into how Sony handled similar problems with *Everquest* (Taylor 2006), it was determined that *WoW*'s stringent rules on erotic role-play are most likely the result of wanting to avoid negative media attention or punishment from the law or the Entertainment Software Review Board. The result of the ban on erotic role-play is not that the behaviour was stopped altogether but that players had found ways to tactically use built-in game functions to get around the rules. Whisper and party-chat functions reappropriated their intended use as tools for accomplishing combat objectives and became a way to erotic role-play without attracting the attention of the game masters.

In the absence of official rules on sexuality, it was discovered the *World of Warcraft* guild and players created their own. Of specific importance were rules that sought to limit the crossover between in-character and out-of-character erotic play. Not only did the guild create and maintain an official rule that attempted to keep the two separate but participants Greenhat and Penpy both created and implemented their own rules to ensure that they and their partners kept ERP within the diegetic frame. Penpy's rules in particular were analysed as an attempt to manage his subjection to multiple sexual economies. The analysis of these rules made reference back to Foucault's (1984) idea that sexual austerity is key in modern understandings of the care of the self and erotic role-play provides a laterally different economy of sexuality that encourages exploration. So while the playful environment of a game invites sexuality to be played with and explored, players developed their own rules to ensure the sexual-play experience stayed out of their primary social frame and had limited access to their sense of self. The creation of rules to keep the two separate was analysed as being indicative of a larger paradox within play and sexuality. On the one hand, play opens the exploration of non-normative sexuality through its frivolous and not serious nature and on the other, rules, even those that are self-imposed, place limitations on how subversive these explorations can be outside the game.

Furthermore, this chapter has provided context and justification for erotic role-play to be considered a part of a game. The rules involved in shaping erotic role-play help to differentiate its gameness from otherwise sexual or erotic behaviours. This is to say, rather than merely adapting a playful attitude towards sexuality, as referred to by Brian Sutton-Smith's (2001) account of playing hide the thimble, sex as understood by erotic role-players becomes folded into the game. The endogenous and diegetic rules, which govern both what is possible and appropriate, envelops erotic role-play as part of the game through its positioning of goals. Be the goal character development, diegetic realness, enhancement of a plot, or silly fun with friends, the official and player-created rules of erotic role-play structure it as part of a game through the importance placed on the activity's functionality within gaming systems. Rather than have an end goal of physical sexual pleasure, as might be assumed of Sutton-Smith's adult play or cybersex, the goals of erotic role-play always reference back to the larger goals of role-playing games. By thinking about erotic role-play as part of a game, rather than just behaviour or play, insight is provided into the kinds of meanings attributed to the activity by its players: that it largely exists and remains within the diegetic frame. Keeping the power of rules to structure play in mind, the following chapter will continue the exploration into how erotic role-players contribute meanings to their play by focusing on the out-of-character relationships that develop.

NOTES

1. A seduction check is a mechanic that uses dice-rolling to determine the statistical probability of one character seducing another. The next paragraph gives a more in-depth explanation.
2. The following chapter will further elaborate on potential crossover effects between frames, so for now the focus will remain on rules.
3. For more information, see: http://us.battle.net/wow/en/forum/topic/4661686614.
4. Video found at http://www.youtube.com/watch?v=UVknVfIW-z0.
5. The issue of privacy and anonymity of participants is called into question when easily identifiable locations in the game are mentioned. However, the name of the server is omitted. Additionally, none of the participants reported visiting Goldshire. It is only included here for discussion because of its centrality to Blizzard's plan of action against ERP.
6. Reader opinions can be found at the end of the article: http://wow.joystiq.com/2010/08/04/blizzard-to-patrol-moon-guards-goldshire-for-harassment-erotic/.
7. The massive multiplayer element of *World of Warcraft* allows for a diversity of chat options. Players may whisper one other player and have a private conversation, they may use party chat to talk to up to four other players, guild chat to speak with only members of their guild, or one of the public general chats to talk to the entire server.
8. For an in-depth account of the differences between cybersex and erotic role-play, see the end of section four in Chapter Three.

9. The 'need' Greenhat refers to involves a system for the distribution of treasure after a battle. A window pops up on the user's interface detailing the item and players can either click 'greed' if they would like to have it or 'need' if they feel their character would benefit from it more than the other characters in the group. If a player selects 'need' on everything, they are said to be a 'ninja', which refers to sneakily and unfairly taking items out of greed.

6 ERP IRL

It is often assumed that because participants claim sexual play in virtual worlds is one of the highlights of their time spent online, as in the works of Boellstorff (2008) and Turkle (1995), erotic activities experienced there will directly cross over into the flesh by means of physical arousal. Within role-play communities there is also an assumption that erotic role-players are simply looking for a cheap thrill. The ways in which erotic role-players play with carnal pleasures in an environment of manageable risk seem to upset other players' normative ideas of what constitutes appropriate sexual behaviour.

As evidenced in the previous chapter's take on the Terms of Use of *World of Warcraft*, erotic role-play often garners disapproval from others in the role-playing community. The terms 'crossover' or 'bleed' themselves seem to be used within role-playing communities as a cautionary term that warns players to not confuse the boundaries between the real and the virtual/ imaginary. Such a term, and its reliance on binary separation, is built into the negative stereotypes of erotic role-players as thrill-seekers and masturbators. From fieldwork, I learned that good role-players and erotic role-players are able to separate their own sexual desire from their characters and manage the effects of crossover. However, in this chapter I upset this binary assumption by demonstrating the pleasures derived from erotic role-play are diverse and the ratio of carnal and imaginary in them is variable. Central to this demonstration is the idea that all pleasure, even in real sex, is derived through an interaction of body and mind.

I identify three modalities within participant responses that exemplify the various ways erotic role-players gain pleasure from the act. The first example comes from an interview excerpt in which Priscilla answers the question of whether or not arousal and masturbation are the primary reasons she erotic role-plays. Her response, which centres on the importance of character-building and story, is read as a modality of the contemplative reader who is active in their erotic role-play. This response is countered by referencing the stereotypical assumptions of the tabletop group, who insist the virtual nature of erotic role-play online allows for carnality to be experienced at the expense of good role-playing. The second modality comes from Megan and Caleb who use erotic role-play to experiment with sexual acts not found in their routine sexual behaviour. They then draw on the insights gained from their activities to influence their real sexual acts by pointing out their imagination is involved in both. The third and final modality comes from Dirty, who, out of all the participants, most closely resembles the stereotype of the erotic role-player who uses the activity to masturbate. In his retelling of his favourite erotic role-play experience, however, he troubles the binary separation between real and virtual/imaginary by questioning my own use of the term 'real' during the interview. For Dirty, who partook in similar activities in real life as in erotic role-play, the boundaries between real and virtual/imaginary seemed arbitrary at best. Through this modality it becomes clear that even for participants who seem to fulfil the stereotype of online erotic role-players as thrill-seekers and masturbators, the activity is nuanced within a larger context of out-of-game sexual behaviours.

As the previous chapter established, erotic role-play affords players a bounded space of manageable risk in which to experiment with types of sexuality outside their routine behaviour. Section two of this chapter, however, points out that however manageable risk in erotic role-play might be, there are still risks that must be contended with. In erotic role-play, the switching of frames involved in the activity can be psychologically difficult to manage, challenges are raised for monogamy, and there is potential for players' out-of-character emotions to become involved. To help manage these risks, players employed humour and mutual surveillance as management strategies. Additionally, the use of these strategies is reflected in terms of intimacy. It was discovered management strategies were less prevalent within groups of participants who had tackled issues of emotionality and comfort with their fellow players in other frames. If the participant erotic role-played with people they were concurrently physically intimate with, humour and surveillance were less present as strategies of managing risk. This is evidenced by a comparison between two accounts from Scott and Dan. In Scott's account of one of his first role-playing sessions, humour and surveillance were used to manage the potential emotional risks, whereas these strategies did not feature in Dan's account of erotic role-playing within a group he was already sexually intimate with.

The third and final section of this chapter assesses what relationships, if any, developed between erotic role-play partners because of the activity. Although it might be assumed, given the sexualised nature of ERP, romantic relationships might develop out-of-character through in-character interactions, this was not found to be the case. All participants discussed building platonic friendships with their erotic role-play partner(s). Through observed gift exchanges and interview data about communication outside the game, this section argues friendships that develop through erotic role-play are similar to friendships that develop from any other hobby. The presence of erotic content seems to factor little in the nature or development of the friendships.

MULTIPLE PLEASURES

No research exists that explores the relationship between online and offline sexual practices for erotic role-players. Because of this, this section is based primarily on interview and focus-group responses to a question asking whether or not erotic role-play has ever led to physical arousal or sexual excitement. The three modalities previously mentioned are presented as varieties of the relationship between in-game, role-played sex, and out-of-game embodied pleasure. The first modality, which is indicative of the contemplative reader who actively chooses when and how to involve erotic content into role-play, is exemplified by Priscilla's response to the interview question asking if physical arousal is the primary reason she erotic role-plays. Instead of focusing on arousal, her response focuses on the pleasure found within developing personal connections to her character and her partner.

> PRISCILLA: No. I enjoy the ability to connect on a personal level as my character with her partner. I think sex is a very natural part of real life, and it makes sense for my character to also actively participate in it, whether or not I am at the moment driven by sexual desire.

Priscilla describes her enjoyment of erotic role-play as one based on a need for consistency within the construct of a fictional world in which relationships have meaning. For her to perform erotic role-play and derive pleasure from the experience, she must feel a diegetically real consistency between the activities undertaken by her character in the game world and her own idea of how relationships function. For Priscilla to role-play a character in a relationship, there must be sexuality present for the relationship to feel meaningful and for Priscilla to 'connect on a personal level' to her character and her character's partner. The absence of sexuality from character relationships would be inconsistent with Priscilla's view that 'sex is a very natural part of real life'. Role-playing character relationships would not be as satisfying for Priscilla if it lacked an erotic component, which she feels is 'natural' and integral to developing personal connections.

The importance Priscilla places on the personal connections developed by her character and their role in her enjoyment of erotic role-play demonstrate how erotic role-play can exist independently from physical arousal or desire and form a different type of pleasure. For Priscilla, whether or not she is 'at the moment driven by sexual desire' does not factor into her decision to erotic role-play. Rather, her decision is influenced by whether or not sexual activities would make sense for her character and her character's relationships at the time it is suggested. This not only highlights the perspective that erotic role-play is not always about thrill-seeking and carnal pleasure but also points out some erotic role-players find pleasure in the contemplative and active syncopation between their personal views of sex and relationships outside the game and the actions and behaviours of their characters inside it. The pleasure from this reflects a consistency within personal beliefs of how relationships are formed and managed and how this contributes to a diegetically believable experience. Priscilla's emphasis on diegetic realness at the expense of her own sexual desires clashes with the stereotypical idea that erotic role-play occurs only for carnal pleasure. Additionally, this is typical of participant definitions of good role-playing, in that Priscilla makes a clear distinction between her own wants and desires and that of her character. Priscilla's clashing with stereotypes and the fact her behaviour might be viewed as good role-playing conflicts with the opinions the tabletop group had of online erotic role-players.

So far virtuality has only been discussed as an abstract concept concerned with simulation and the imagination. However, the tabletop participants understood the virtual nature of erotic role-play in *World of Warcraft* in the popular use of the term, making reference to computer-mediated, virtual worlds and realities. They used virtuality to differentiate their offline role-play from online erotic role-players by relying on the perceived differences in anonymity offered by erotic role-playing in virtual worlds. During the focus group, I asked Joe, Scott, and Dan whether arousal and masturbation were the primary reasons they involved erotic themes in their tabletop sessions. They responded negatively, however, and they additionally took the question as an opportunity to differentiate their erotic role-play from the online variety through describing the difference in medium. From their perspective, erotic role-play in online virtual worlds is primarily done for the players' out-of-character pleasure.

> DAN: With all due respect, it seems like with that type of role-playing, it is more about getting your rocks off than anything else. I mean, whereas I've used that sort of thing, to be honest, it probably sounds more frequent than it is. Sex doesn't come up all that often and we're talking in a career [in role-playing] that has now spanned 15 years.
> JOE: And we picked out specific points.
> SCOTT: I think in mine it has only come up 7 or 8 times.
> DAN: More for me, vastly more. But it does seem like in online role-playing a lot revolves around sex, with all the other aspects being sacrificed to that, which I can't say I'm too happy with.
> SCOTT: [Pretending to be an online erotic role-player.] "Yay! My wank can involve someone else!"

Although Joe, Scott, and Dan do not regularly play *World of Warcraft* or another MMORPG, they have tried to do so in the past. From the interview excerpt as well as observational notes, the topic of role-playing in virtual worlds only came up a few times. Every time it was brought up, however, the tabletop participants made efforts to distinguish themselves as different from online erotic role-players through their difference in motivations to erotic role-play. In their view, erotic role-play in online virtual worlds is done only as a masturbation aid, whereas they view the erotic role-play they involve in their tabletop scenes as directly contributing to the game in some way. Although Joe, Scott, and Dan's perception of erotic role-play online conflicts with how the *World of Warcraft* participants in the first modality view the act, it provides insight into differences between the mediums used for erotic role-play. The anonymity and privacy offered through computer-mediated ERP was viewed by the tabletop group as creating an environment in which physical sexuality could occur through masturbation. As previously alluded to in the interview excerpt with Priscilla, however, erotic role-play did not usually lead to sexual activity or even influence the types of sexual activities participants engaged with in-the-flesh. In the following interview excerpt, Megan and Caleb reflect on the relationship between their erotic stories and their in-the-flesh behaviour and discuss the medium of expressing sexuality through text and how it is different from real life.

> CALEB: As I see it, writing some smutty stories is nothing really excessively kinky compared to what we actually do in our own bedroom.
> INTERVIEWER: I thought you both said you're mundane?
> CALEB: Well, in our daily life.
> MEGAN: Well, yeah, but real sex is naughtier than fake sex!
> CALEB: And that. Reality trumps fantasy every time. Even if the fantasy is the most absurdly over the top kink, it's still just imagination. We don't equate fantasy with reality. In fact, there's no conversion rate. Thoughts are just that.

In the excerpt, Caleb focuses first on establishing his and Megan's in-the-flesh sexual activities are kinkier than the stories they write. Previously in the interview, both he and Megan had described themselves as 'mundane and otherwise average when it came to sexual experimentation in their lives outside of the game. I questioned his use of the term 'kinky' and the relationship it has to the previous assertion of being mundane. In the responses that followed, both Megan and Caleb asserted 'reality trumps fantasy every time'. Their clear separation between reality and fantasy can be read as not only emphasising the limits they place on the medium – that textual erotic role-play is 'just imagination', unlike real sex – but also they are subjecting themselves to two different economies of pleasure. That which is kinky or naughty in their co-authored fiction is different from that which is kinky or naughty in their in-the-flesh sexual activities. The pleasure Megan and Caleb get out of erotic role-play forms the second modality that can be summarised as an experimentation that provides insight. Through their experimentation with alternate sexual activities in the imaginary game world, they reflect on their out-of-game sexual activities and ultimately find there is 'no conversion rate'. However, as will be seen later in this chapter, the topics, themes, and actions they experiment with in erotic role-play function as a type of rehearsal or foreplay for future sexual acts. Ultimately, the pleasure Megan and Caleb find in erotic role-play is through the invocation of thoughts and imagination that may lead to arousal but certainly lead to creative expression via the creation of erotic stories, which is pleasurable in itself. Like Priscilla, Megan's and Caleb's delineation of erotic role-play as just thoughts seems to be at odds with the stereotypical idea that erotic role-players are only interested in the act as a carnal endeavour.

Megan and Caleb's comparison between fantasy erotic role-play and imagination and thoughts is read as indicative of a necessary presence of a certain virtuality in real sex. That is to say, if we define virtuality as a type of imaginary, simulational, alternate reality by way of Poster (1995), the virtual can be found in participants' in-the-flesh sex just as easily as in erotic role-play. Likewise, a few participants mentioned in the interviews that physical reality, by way of arousal and masturbation, did occur during or after a virtual sexual performance. The most pertinent example of this comes through one particular interview with Old Dirty Troll. When asked to recount his favourite erotic role-play experience, he reflected on a time in which a crossover from the game world to in-the-flesh sexual behaviour occurred. From erotic role-playing within the game to using voice-chat software to indicate out-of-character pleasure, the following account helps to illustrate the futility in attempts to separate the virtual from the real and the mind from the body in erotic role-play and comprises the third modality of pleasure discussed in this section.

DIRTY: Basically there were two ladies that [Character] was friends with, and is still friends with them. They flirted with him quite a bit, you know, big troll guy, and them being blood elves. Well he finally had enough and carried them both off.

INTERVIEWER: Literally carried them off?

DIRTY: Oh yeah, when he wants a woman or women, he takes them. He is definitely an alpha troll male. Shares that characteristic with his player. Very blunt when we want something. Well suffice to say we all got pretty hot with the session, one of the ladies had never ERPed or done anything sexual with another female and was very submissive to both myself and the other female player. I'm very descriptive when I ERP, I like it to be as real and visceral as possible, and they got off on that big time. Soooo not sure how it happened, but the recommendation of going on my [voice chat] server happened and we moved from in-game to Vent[1] and started telling each other what our characters were doing while, er, we all got each other off. [It] was pretty fucking hot.

INTERVIEWER: And everyone stayed in-character the whole time?

DIRTY: Yeah, well, LOL, minus the usual sounds people make while masturbating and such.

INTERVIEWER: This may be inappropriate to ask, but have you ever done something like that in real life?

DIRTY: You mean with multiple partners?

INTERVIEWER: Yeah.

DIRTY: Yep. I'm into the BDSM lifestyle, so kink is fairly normal.

INTERVIEWER: Ah, I see.

DIRTY: Not saying I'm a porn star or anything, but I've had the pleasure of doing that sort of thing a few times.

In Dirty's account of his favourite erotic role-play experience, we see multiple pleasures crossing over from in-game erotic role-play to in-the-flesh speech and auditory sounds of pleasure. Through the use of voice-chat software, Dirty and his partners moved their in-game, in-character actions into the flesh by using their own voices to describe what their characters were doing as well as to express the 'usual sounds people make while masturbating'. Whether or not masturbation actually occurred is irrelevant. By lending their voices to describe what their characters were doing, the participants changed the textual medium through which erotic role-play was experienced. The change of medium affected the nature of the communication within the experience. In particular, this seems to have precipitated a switch from the diegetic frame to a blurring with the primary social frame. Quite telling of this shift is Dirty asking for clarification by what I meant by 'real life'. For him, this experience transgressed the boundary of virtual and real when it moved from the game's text to verbal communication. So although the excerpt from Dirty is closest to what might be considered the stereotypical, masturbatory response to erotic role-play, it still conflates binaries between virtuality and reality. In the movement from the game world into voice-chat software while still staying in-character, Dirty involved both his body, through the use of voice to indicate masturbatory sounds and descriptions of actions, and the mind, through collaborative storytelling without the visual aids of the virtual world.

Perhaps most similar to the tabletop group's method of orally articulating erotic scenes, the change in the media used by Dirty and his partners can be read as a partial relinquishing of anonymity. This further conflates the stereotypical expectation that the anonymity afforded by ERPing online lends itself more easily to playing with sexuality for the sake of carnal pleasure. In using their voice to describe the actions of their characters, the players released some information about themselves such as perceived gender and age and accents. This can be read alongside Dirty's admission he had a friendship with the other two characters and has experienced similar activities in-the-flesh to hint at the importance of familiarity in moving erotic role-play from online to offline. The idea that out-of-game familiarity with either partners or sexual acts influences the crossover between erotic role-play and in-the-flesh sexual activities will be explored further in the next section.

STRATEGIES

As previously argued, erotic role play in imaginary worlds provides players with an environment of manageable risks to experiment with sexuality. However, this does not mean the activity is risk free. In addition to issues of anonymity, which participants attempt to manage through the creation of rules, there are additional risks that arise from the activity. The switching of frames, for example, is fraught with psychological implications, and intrinsic to any discussion of sexuality are risks of discomfort and embarrassment. Furthermore, as detailed in Penpy's account of a situation that began to compromise his monogamy, there is the risk real emotions and attachments will develop and these might lead to conflicting feelings or complications in other relationships. In addition to the already discussed use of rules, other individual strategies were developed to help maximise the comfort of participants while minimising their perceived risk to self. In particular, humour and mutual surveillance emerged from interview data and observations as being strategies to minimise the risks to the self that may crossover from the virtual world and into the real.

In the first excerpt, Scott recalls an experience from his past in response to a question that asked how long he had been role-playing. In the focus group, he noted this was one of his first experiences with tabletop role-playing and one of his first experiences role-playing with erotic themes. In the excerpt, humour emerges as a strategy to minimise the risk of embarrassment when discussing sexual themes.

> SCOTT: I just remember one group I was in when I was in college. I would have been about sixteen or seventeen. It was the only group I've been in where it was all women and it was the most sex-obsessed chronicle I've ever known to be run in the most hideously tongue-in-cheek way. I mean, that group had a character that was meant to be an unstable dark cleric who, well [the player's] description of her character was: 'looks roughly like Michael Jackson, but whenever you look at him you can't help but think of badgers'. At which point, it was fantastic. He'd scream like a girl when charging into battle and do a manly war cry to flee from things. It was fantastic. And [he] was regularly caught masturbating.

In Scott's description of a campaign he was in years ago, sexual themes were treated in a largely frivolous and silly way. The sexuality and gender of one particular character were played with in a 'tongue-in-cheek' manner. While the age of the group and the overall tone of the game undoubtedly influenced the performance of the character, I believe the intimacy of the group also influenced how sexual themes were treated. Scott had not been playing with this group for long and was not romantically involved with any of the players. I interpret the silly and frivolous nature of the dark cleric's sexuality as done in order to keep the themes of sexuality comfortable through humour. Humour is used here as a means of distancing the topics at play away from the sensibilities found in the primary social framework. By laughing at the sexuality as it is portrayed, any perceived threats to the players' sense of sexual ethics outside the game world can be managed. In this case, humour additionally functioned as a type of mutual surveillance. By presenting sexual themes in a humorous context, the role-players in Scott's first group set a precedent for that particular campaign, which mandated that sexual themes be treated frivolously. The effect of the strategy of enforcing humour presumably provided comfort to the topic of sexuality by disarming potentially embarrassing themes through laughter. If a player were to attempt to invoke serious sexuality in such a campaign, the others would likely attempt to subvert it into a type of joke. By looking at other participant accounts of erotic role-play scenarios, the role mutual surveillance plays in dictating the types of content available for play and how these types of play cross over into the participants' real lives becomes clearer.

As the following interview excerpt will show, players' relationship statuses greatly influenced how they applied their experiential knowledge of erotic role-play or even whether or not they erotic role-played at all. Although it might be tempting to think erotic role-play might be more popular with single, unattached players, this was not always the case. Dan explains the only time he played out sexual scenes was when he was with a group of players he was also sexually involved with. In such a scenario, the out-of-game intimacy between participants minimised the need for distancing strategies such as humour.

> DAN: My first-ever character had a, well, it was a sort of platonic-sexual relationship, not really sexual at all. Um, after that it didn't really enter into [the game] too much. If it happened, it happened off camera until I got really heavily into White Wolf gaming, and more specifically got into a group with people I was actually fucking at the time. That was when we started getting characters like [Dan's favourite character] who was a gay Child of Gaia, whose sex actually happened on camera as it were.

For Dan, explicit scenes only happened in a role-play group he was concurrently intimate with at the time. Although he had implied scenes with past groups, it was after he had become sexually intimate outside of the game that he began bringing sex into the game. I interpret this to be indicative of the level of comfort and intimacy required to describe an erotic scene in-the-flesh. Because of the nature of tabletop role-playing, which requires players be in close physical proximity and communicate face to face, meaningful and emotional scenes in erotic role-play scenarios with strangers often become uncomfortable. This is not to suggest the *World of Warcraft* participants do not struggle with this discomfort as well, rather that the perceived anonymity of the format makes it easier to ignore. I propose that one of the reasons silly and frivolous sex is introduced into games is to manage the feelings and emotions associated with the switching of frames. In the first example from Scott, in which he lacked Dan's level of intimacy with his fellow players, keeping potentially damaging emotions attached to sexuality distanced from the primary social frame was important for the group's comfort. In Dan's case, in which sexuality had already been experienced in multiple other frames, role-playing with sexual themes in a group setting required less frame management. Dan's group could afford to be less vigilant in maintaining the boundaries between frames because sexual activity within the group was already experienced in multiple frames. In this case, the risks of embarrassment or the development of emotional attachments needed to be contended with in other frames, thus minimising the need to manage the diegetic or player frames in particular.

Similarly, one way some of the *World of Warcraft* couples in this study overcame emotional management between frames was to erotic role-play together. Rather than create a relationship for themselves or their characters, two couples in this study who lived together discussed ERP as something that happened organically and was folded into their relationship. Without prompting, both couples described themselves as having an active and healthy sex life outside the game. Before they discovered erotic role-play in *World of Warcraft*, Grin and Lamb discussed their use of erotic fiction, while Megan and Caleb discussed their use of adult chatrooms. In both cases, these alternate methods of arousal and foreplay were folded into their mutual sexual behaviour. When they started playing *World of Warcraft*, they simply transitioned to using erotic role-play to fulfil a similar function. Below are two excerpts that highlight the functional role of ERP in their in-the-flesh sexual activities:

> INTERVIEWER: Have you ever engaged in sex with each other directly after an ERP session?
> GRIN: Bedroom madness would always follow, lol.
> LAMB: Yes and yes.
> MEGAN: We mostly think of ERP with others as 'practice' for one another, a way to tease one another (ie. sending each other the chatlogs) or as a way to get turned on for the other person.

For the couples, erotic role-play served a function similar to foreplay. Like the second modality described in section one of this chapter, erotic role-play provided experimental sexual insights into what the participants found erotic. Exploring sexual themes through their characters and play was a 'way to get turned on for the other person', with the understanding that 'bedroom madness' would follow once the ERP session was finished. Absent from these accounts is the use of humour as a strategy for managing comfort when discussing sexual themes. Through my interpretation of Grin, Lamb, and Megan's responses, combined with Dan's earlier insight involving descriptive erotic scenes in tabletop, I found previously established intimacy between participants minimised the need to manage emotions that developed in separate frames. Rather than needing to separate erotic role-play as a bounded space for exploration, they were willing to fold it into part of their sexual practice[2].

In this section's participant accounts of erotic role-play, several larger points are made about how players can explore non-normative sexuality in their play. In Scott's account, humour and mutual surveillance were used to manage potentially risky emotions, such as attachment or embarrassment, when playing with non-normative gender expressions and sexual themes within groups that lacked established intimacy in other frames. These strategies, however, were not found in examples where participants were already sexually intimate with their erotic role-play partners. This suggests tools used to separate boundaries between the frames of player and character are not in place when participants are comfortable and intimate with their ERP partners. Presumably this is because in such situations, issues of intimacy and familiarity are already being contended with in multiple other frames. With a minimised need to manage risks between frames, ERP was able to cross over both emotionally and physically in the case of Grin, Lamb, Megan, and Caleb. In the following section, participant responses relating to the types of friendships that evolved through their erotic role-play will be discussed.

FRIENDSHIPS

As the last two sections provided evidence against a binary relationship between carnality and imagination, this section furthers the argument by pointing out the role of friendships in erotic role-playing. Just as stereotypical assumptions about the purpose of ERP tend to focus on physical carnality or masturbation, the development of a romantic relationship between players is also assumed to be a significant motivation or side effect. However, just as previous responses troubled the binary between virtual actions and physical reactions, participant responses and observational data point out the pleasures that develop from erotic role-playing make redundant a binary separation between romantic and platonic relationship categories. Similar to other hobbies, such as joining a sports team or political group, the real significance of ERP lies in the development of friendship networks. These networks additionally question normative assumptions about the need to separate romantic from platonic with a view that such distinctions are a part of a discursive-disciplinary apparatus that seeks to valorise real sexual relationships as they function within a social and political system. By abstracting themselves from an economy of pleasure that operates on the binary assumptions of such a system, a greater fluidity of relationships and the meanings they contain are afforded to erotic role-players.

During fieldwork, I observed some of the *World of Warcraft* participants traded screen names, phone numbers, and e-mail addresses in guild chat so they could communicate with one another outside the game. Because logging into the game requires a computer that meets specific hardware requirements as well as a fast Internet connection, player communication in-game during work days was often limited. The guild's forum was one way in which participants kept in touch with one another. Some of the participants with smart phones would regularly post on the forum during lunch breaks or during long public commutes. Other participants with office jobs would routinely check the forums while at work. Participants wishing to communicate with ERP partners not in the guild used other methods of communication. During one interview, I asked Greenhat if she still kept in touch with one of her ERP partners. In her response, she describes using an instant messenger service to chat with the other player.

> GREENHAT: Yeah after I started a relationship with the person and deemed them safe we exchanged [AOL Instant Messenger IDs] and continued to RP out there to further develop the characters' interactions. We were friends for several years. Still talk with her. She's married to her best friend.

In the excerpt, Greenhat describes how she had to first conduct a risk assessment on her erotic role-play partner before she went on to share out-of-game information. In the previous chapter, Greenhat discussed the rules and processes she had created to screen potential ERP partners before booking them in for a session. Similar to Scott's example in section two, this risk assessment is another example of a surveillance strategy used to minimise potential emotional and psychological issues that might arise from switching frames. Greenhat's concern for security can be seen as flexible in this example. After she deems the other person 'safe', she is willing to negotiate her privacy and anonymity for a more personal, friendly connection to the other player. Although this negotiation might be identified as a type of disclosure, it perhaps better relates to the idea of 'mutual receptivity' (Blatterer 2013, p. 5), in that it not only represents a mutual agreement to disclose contact information but also a receptiveness to the development of a relational construction of self within the friendship. This is perhaps most clearly witnessed in Greenhat's detailing of how she and her ERP partner used instant relay chat to further develop their characters' interactions. The use of an external chat program to plan and execute character interactions is indicative not only of mutual story-telling but also of receptiveness to the wants and desires of the player at the other end of the screen.

In addition to the assumption that the stereotypical erotic role-player uses the activity for carnal pleasure is the assumption that online relationships and friendships lack the substance and meaningfulness of their in-the-flesh counterparts. Previous research into online social networking websites has found a need for 'emotional reflexivity' as everyday contacts are sorted by the 'strength' of their relationship offline (Holmes 2011). Likewise, the idea of out-of-game friendships developing through in-game interactions has been observed in past studies on MMORPGs. In T.L. Taylor's (2006) ethnographic research on *Everquest,* she found many players who met in-game then developed friendships that would often be taken outside the game, even going as far as meeting in-the-flesh at official conventions or informal guild events. Like Mary Holmes' (2011) research on social media outlets, Taylor's observation relies on in-the-flesh meetings to legitimise friendships that emerged from online interactions. Greenhat's interview excerpt, however, provides evidence for overturning the binary distinctions between online and offline relationships. In moving her conversations from the game world to an auxiliary communication platform that was still online, Greenhat's experience may be viewed as strengthening her friendship through additional opportunities for contact without needing to meet in-the-flesh. The need to distinguish between online and offline communication as a platform for relationship building is minimised in cases like Greenhat's, which have more commonalities with real relationships than the stereotype of virtual ones. Like offline social connections, Greenhat's friendship with her erotic role-play partner required upkeep and maintenance. She notes she was friends with her ERP partner for several years but uses the past tense to indicate she no longer defines the relationship as a friendship through a drop in frequency of communication. Like offline acquaintances, Greenhat and her partner now chat only occasionally to update one another when a major life event, such as a marriage, occurs.

Unlike Greenhat and her erotic role-play partner, the tabletop participants did not begin their friendship specifically through role-playing. However, like Greenhat, they did bond and build their friendship through role-playing. During the focus group, I asked how the tabletop participants met and they responded they were all members of a similar social circle for reasons other than role-playing. It was when a mutual friend tried to introduce Scott and Dan as potential romantic partners that they began talking about role-play.

> SCOTT: It's through [mutual friend] I met you, then I found out you're a role-player, and then I went, "YOU! This way!"
> DAN: [Giggling] Yes, I think [mutual friend] tried to set me up with Scott and the conversation basically went, "Ah yes, I hear you are a role-player. Ah yes, let us play role-playing games!"
> Everyone chuckles.

SCOTT: And [mutual friend] sighed because it meant nothing dirty was going to happen and just walked off as we just nerded at each other.

DAN: [Laughing] Yeah!

INT: Was this at a club?

JOE: [Laughing] No, it was at a house party.

SCOTT: [Laughing] It was at a house party. A very drunken house party!

After their initial meet at a house party, Joe, Scott, and Dan began role-playing together on a semi-regular basis. Occasionally, a visiting or interested friend would drop in for one session or even an entire campaign, but Joe, Scott, and Dan comprised the group's core members. During the observation period, I noted that multiple times a week I would get a text message sent by Scott concerning the upcoming role-play session. Likewise, it was not uncommon for Scott, Dan, or Joe to meet up during the week to discuss plans for the campaign. Aside from providing an opportunity to talk about the game, these meet-ups also provided an opportunity for sociali-sation and chat about general life events. Although the tabletop group exclusively role-played in-the-flesh, their use of text messaging to plan and discuss future role-play sessions resembles Greenhat's use of instant relay chat to fulfil the same function. In both cases text, computer-mediated messages were sent to further develop plots between characters as well as plan future events. Additionally, both methods of textual communication led to out-of-character socialisation with ensuing chats about participants' personal lives. This observational data helps to further question the binary separation of online and offline or virtual and real, because the textual communication achieved similar end results: the strengthening of social bonds through out-of-game and out-of character communication.

Also during the participant observation period of the research, I observed both groups of participants gave and received gifts. For the tabletop group, this was done in a casual way largely unrelated to the game itself. For example, the participants would occasionally bring beer, liquor, soft drinks, and snacks to share with each other. The gaming sessions would occasionally reflect special occasions like Christmas and birthdays, with the exchange of presents happening before the game commenced. These gifts ranged from engraved pocket watches to expensive bottles of rum and sometimes new or special-edition rulebooks of the games they played. During the focus group, however, none of the participants discussed these gifts or gestures. Perhaps this is because they viewed the acts as normative within a larger cultural context of propriety; it is customary to give a present to someone celebrating a birthday, for example. Gift-giving has long been established as a socio-economic exchange used to gain, demonstrate, and reaffirm social connections (Mauss 1990; Belk and Coon 1993). Specifically in sociology, the giving of gifts has been viewed as a normative behaviour centred on reciprocity (Gouldner 1960). Because the participants in this study are all from similar cultural and economic backgrounds, I interpret their gift exchanges as both a part of a larger cultural imperative that mandates gifts be given on special occasions and also as indicative of friendships that have crossed over from the player frame into participants' primary social frame.

The digital nature of *World of Warcraft* surprisingly changes very little to the concept of giving presents. In-character birthdays, weddings, and births were all marked by a celebration and gift exchange. Likewise, the Feast of Winterveil, an in-game holiday celebrated during Chanukah, Christmas, and Kwanza, ritualised the exchange of brightly wrapped presents between characters. Participants also reported giving and receiving gifts of flowers, sweets, and jewellery during courtship, and, for special occasions, rare pets, mounts, and in-character clothing. Out-of-character, players would often mark their birthday on the guild calendar and occasionally host informal birthday parties over voice-chat software.

Although characters sent each other gifts in the game, the majority of gifts exchanged between players were non-material. Blizzard's website facilitates player-to-player exchange by purchasing digital, download-able goods such as game time or special pets, but despite this, none of the participants in this study reported giving or receiving these types of gifts. Specifically, gifts exchanged between ERP partners most often took the form of art or stories that depicted erotic scenes between the charac-ters involved. Belk and Coon (1993) rationalise this homemade practice by stating, "One indicant that some informants esteem dating gifts for their symbolic value rather than their economic value is that nonmaterial gifts are often perceived as more desirable than material gifts" (p. 403). Aside from desirability, there are other factors that might contribute to the exchange of crafted gifts.

First, the physical distance between players often complicates how easily gifts can be exchanged. Some participants chose to keep their real-world identities private, which created an impeding barrier to the gift-exchange process. Greenhat, for example, confessed to knowing very little about the player of her character's life-mate. She wrote, "I know she's a good player, that she's a she and a couple of other small details but we don't talk about it much. I can tell she's not comfortable revealing such information so I just keep it as comfortable as possible". For a variety of reasons, some players choose to remain anonymous no matter how familiar they become with their online partners or how much they socialise with the guild.

Second, the creation and development of a romantic relationship between avatars is often difficult to imagine and describe without the use of external visual representations like drawings. The customisation options for avatars in *World of Warcraft* are limited, which is often frustrating for role-players who want their characters' physical appearance to match their unique story. Just as previous research has noted fans of popular television shows and games will often create and share artwork and stories about favourite characters to express and demonstrate their individual interpretations

(Jenkins 2006; Griffiths 2003), so too do *World of Warcraft* players. Often, add-on software is used to give characters unique descriptions that are impossible to represent within the graphics of the game. Scars, injuries, piercings, tattoos, and other physical descriptors are included to enrich the visual representation of the character. Players often find it frustrating when there is either not enough space provided to fully describe their character or when they are limited by the use of language to fully explain their character's appearance. The guild's forums, for example, contain several discussion threads for players to post lengthy written descriptions, artwork depicting their characters, or photos of celebrities and models that encapsulate some aspect of their character's appearance. The goal of these threads is to help other players see a character as their player imagines them. For this reason, stories and artwork that feature the intricacies of a character's appearance as the player has defined it are highly valued gifts. Although such gifts may be consider non-material, in that they lack a direct economic exchange value and are given and received through digital media, they further blur the binary separation between online and offline friendships by adapting an established offline social practice for online use. Furthermore, if we are to understand gifts given as an extension of the giver and the reception of gifts as the symbolic acceptance of the giver as a person (Mauss 1990; Belk and Coon 1993), then the gift of erotic stories and art tells us much about their value.

Although there are many examples in the interviews of participants co-authoring or exchanging erotic fiction with one another, two examples stood out due to their intensity. Megan and Caleb combined have written over 20 erotic stories involving their *World of Warcraft* characters. The themes of these stories typically involve ideas that the players were uncomfortable enacting in their non-virtual bedroom, such as violent sex and the inclusion of multiple sexual partners. Below is an excerpt from one of Megan and Caleb's stories in which Caleb's character is in a position of power and control over Megan's.

> Pausing, he listened to her cries and touched the knife's blade to her ass cheeks, sliding it up in under the black panties, slicing off one part of the waist band, then over to the other, so that they fell away down to the ground. Pressing his chest and stomach up against her bleeding back, he could feel the heat of her wounds and the warm blood run onto him.
>
> (Excerpt from one of Megan and Caleb's stories)

This story in particular involves Megan's character being chained to a wall, violently whipped, and otherwise subjected to intensely rough sexual acts. During the interview, the couple was asked about their collection of stories, which they had posted semi-publically on the guild's forums. In the interview excerpt below, Caleb describes the function the stories provide in his relationship with Megan.

CALEB: I grew up without a father, surrounded by women I respected, loved and adored. It really made me uncomfortable the notion, even in fantasy, of raping a woman. The first time I tried to 'simulate' (and I use the term very loosely) in bed for Megan, I kinda broke down and had to step away. I couldn't go on in any form; it was far too uncomfortable for me. ... I'm more comfortable with it now. I've cemented the separation in fantasy, I think, so it's no longer a big roadblock for me to do the rape scene stuff in ERP for her.

MEGAN: Any rape story Caleb wrote, he wrote as a gift to me.

The sacrifice and compromise described by Caleb are intense in the expression of the emotional connection he feels to rape, even in a fictional setting. His willingness to use rape in erotic role-play despite his discomfort seems to be tied to his relationship with Megan and a desire to·please her at an emotional cost to himself. Megan's consideration of the stories Caleb writes for her as a 'gift' is consistent with the literature on gift-giving as an extension of the giver (Mauss 1990; Belk and Coon 1993). More than giving the time and skill it takes to write a story, Caleb gifts his emotional compromise in writing about a topic that arouses Megan but he finds problematic.

In another example, Cog wrote a graphic story describing her character's death. Although this was not a gift to any one player in particular, in a way it was a gift to the guild as a whole. The decision to kill a character is not one that is taken lightly. Most players have logged countless hours on their characters, establishing relationships both in and out-of-character along the way. The player undoubtedly develops an emotional attachment to their character under these circumstances. To kill a character is painful, to some degree, to the player and it puts in jeopardy friendships made through the process of role-playing. While in the functional mechanics of the game, character death is relatively common, the role-played death of a character is not. Most avatars will have died during a quest or a dungeon at some point in their career and be resurrected by a spirit healer, the game's mechanic for avoiding the permanent death of a character. In terms of game play, the only negative result of this is damage to the character's armour, which is often costly to repair. These deaths are largely ignored by role-players or adapted into the narrative as a knock out and thus a temporary state of being rendered unconscious. Cog's character, however, was the only character during fieldwork to face a final death. This particular character had been with the guild for at least a year and held several important responsibilities in helping the guild function. The death came as a shock to many players and characters alike. In the story she writes:

A particularly vicious grin tugged at his lips and he slammed himself fully into her, filling her with the efforts of their activities. With his last impaling thrust he leaned up and drove his tusks across the front of her neck. Her eyes shot open and stared down at him thankfully, one of the oddest expressions the Troll had ever seen. "Tell Samedi I send my regards. Jou will not be coming back to take what jou have given, petit pink." With a grunt he pushed the lifeless form of the Elf off of him and gathered himself to bathe and collect what he'd need for the journey that lay ahead.

(Excerpt from Cog's story)

Cog had posted two versions of this story publically on the guild forums. One version, posted for everyone to read, described her character packing her belongings and leaving her home to search out adventures elsewhere. The excerpt above is from the adult version, which was posted in the guild forum's age-restricted section. In this version, the character leaves home to seek out adventures elsewhere but encounters trouble along the way and is murdered. During the interview, Cog discussed the appeal of erotic role-play as resting on the utilisation of her creative skills as a writer and so this story served a double purpose. At once it was a way to provide closure for players concerned about the character and it was a way to provide an end to the character's story.

At several points in the interview, Cog stressed the importance of narrative and of story-creation in her role-playing, and explained she viewed erotic role-play as just one facet of this. But I feel there is something else happening here. Cog could have easily penned this story and kept it to herself if she sought only the completion of a storyline, but instead she posted it publically. While this public posting might have been designed to gather feedback about her skills as an author, I believe it was also a way for her to give closure, at least out-of-character, to other players regarding her character's death. Out of the many stories Cog had written and posted to the forum, I chose to ask about this one in particular during the interview. I asked about the themes present and specifically why she decided to kill her character in such a way.

> COG: Going out the way she lived her life. [Main character] began as a simple and shy bard. A pacifist. When she died was NOTHING like that. She was barely holding onto her sanity, she had been ruined sexually, she had lived to fistfight orcs. I thought it was poetic justice for her to die the way she lived her last months of life.

The response given by Cog reflects her unique emphasis on the continuity of story. The scene she wrote is described in her words as 'poetic justice', a fitting way to end a character's life that had become functionally unplayable due to past events that had 'ruined' her. Like many of the *World of Warcraft* participants, Cog had more than one character in the guild that she regularly played on. Whilst her main character died, she had other characters she could log onto and continue to role-play with the guild. So whilst Cog was guaranteed she would be able to communicate and play with the guild, she still chose to post her story to provide poetic justice for her character's death. I interpret this poetic justice as summarising the character's life and death as a symbolic gesture of closure for her, her friends, and her character's friends. Like Caleb's stories for Megan, I view Cog's story for the guild as a symbolic gesture of friendship that has crossed over from the game into Cog's primary social frame.

Similar to the erotic fiction written by participants, erotic art was also used in gift exchanges. Although some of the art had been commissioned from professional artists, the majority was hand-drawn by the participants themselves. The guild's forums possess a section specifically for sharing and critiquing artwork in which members would share advice, link tutorials, or otherwise provide resources to help their fellow members develop the skill sets required to produce images of their characters. These skills often involved specialist knowledge ranging from the basics of drawing with a pencil and paper to using software programs like Photoshop and Adobe Illustrator. Gifting knowledge and skills allowed artists of varying abilities the opportunity to discuss techniques and styles with others. Of the participants in this study, four had received formal art education and of those four, three currently used their art education in their profession. Priscilla, for example, had no formal art training but was able to create line art for her erotic role-play partner through practice, patience, and suggestions from the guild on how to improve. In this way, the sharing of highly technical and specialised knowledge is a gift in and of itself.

Priscilla's drawing was of her and her partner's characters nude and locked in a loving embrace. When asked about the content of the drawing, Priscilla responded that although it was not a representation of any single ERP session, it was an image indicative of the overall relationship shared with the other character. Rather than e-mailing it privately to her ERP partner, she posted it on the forums in the hope of receiving feedback from other artists as a way to measure the progression of her own skills. When asked during the interview about the drawing, she was keen to receive my feedback. It took great effort to direct her attention away from the stylistic content of the drawing and to focus on her relationship with the other character's player. When I asked if she knew anything about the player, she responded:

> PRISCILLA: I do, we are good friends now OOC [out-of-character] because of our interactions. I have not met him, he doesn't live close to me unfortunately. But we talk every day via [instant messenger] and sometimes over the phone. I'd consider him one of my best friends. He is coming to the wedding. =)

Despite living hundreds of miles apart and never meeting in-the-flesh, Priscilla considers her erotic role-play partner one of her best friends and has even invited him to her wedding. Like Greenhat and the tabletop group, Priscilla mentions she chats to her ERP partner regularly outside the game. Based on her response, the different avenues of communication utilised by her and her partner help to further illustrate that binary distinctions between real and virtual relationships need not be transposed onto the friendships that emerge out of erotic role-play interactions. Although her erotic role-play partner lives across the country, the use of auxiliary communication technology such as telephone calls and text messages bridges gaps in communication normally associated with online friendships and allows for the development of relationality between participants.

In looking at the exchange of presents, money, fiction, and art as symbols of friendship, this section has provided evidence against a stereotype that views erotic role-play as a means to develop romantic relationships. By showing how participants created bonds and friendships with one another, this section showed the social aspect of erotic role-play for players has less to do with sex and more to do with the development of friendships. Rather than viewing technology as an impediment to the development of social networks, it was viewed as providing multiple platforms for communication that were used by both the online and offline erotic role-players. The end result of participants' focus on the building of friendships is a nuanced picture of the act that presents it as most similar to any other hobbyist group. Rather than focus solely on sex, carnal pleasures, and the development of romantic relationships, the friendship-building strategies employed by erotic role-players have been found to be similar to any other hobbyist group. Although participants met their ERP partners under erotic conditions, auxiliary communication took place outside the game world and outside erotic pretences. Just as we might assume a person joining a sports team might develop friendships with other players and communicate about topics other than sports outside matches, so too do erotic role-players.

CONCLUSION

Overall, this chapter helped to overturn stereotypes about erotic role-players and the crossover effects between their in-game activities and out-of-game implications. The first section countered the stereotypical assumption that erotic role-players partake in the activity for carnal pleasure through three modalities in participant responses. These modalities showed not only do participants gain pleasure in multiple ways but additionally the stereotype of erotic role-players rests on a binary divide between real and virtual/imaginary.

The first modality, evidenced by Priscilla as a contemplative reader and actor, demonstrated the pleasure derived from erotic role-play can come from building personal connections through collaborative storytelling. Rather than physical arousal or pleasure, for Priscilla the enjoyment of erotic role-play came from building diegetically believable character relationships. The second modality, as evidenced from Megan's and Caleb's excerpt, found additional pleasure can come from using ERP to experiment with alternate types of sexuality that can then be reflected on outside the game world for arousal. In further commentary in section three, it was noted Megan and Caleb reflect on their co-authored ERP as a way to experiment with ideas and themes they usually find to be both erotic and potentially harmful. Through exploring these ideas and themes in erotic role-play and then reflecting on them later, both Megan and Caleb were able to gain insight into their limits and their desires and found this discovery to be pleasurable. In the third and final modality, Dirty retold his favourite erotic role-play experience that involved the movement from the game world to the real world through the use of voice-chat software to express sounds of arousal and pleasure. Although Dirty may most closely resemble the stereotype of the erotic role-player who uses the activity only for carnal pleasure, his interview responses helped to question the stereotype by pointing out the futility in relying on terms such as virtual and real. Through questioning my use of the term real during the interview, Dirty not only pointed out that he considers his favourite ERP experience to be real but also that binary distinctions between virtuality and reality are unnecessary. Both the body and the mind are active in real and virtual sex.

The second section explored another assumption about erotic role-playing by looking at how risks are managed by participants. As the previous chapter suggested, erotic role-playing, particularly online, is viewed as a bounded space of manageable risks to the self. Because erotic role-play is approached with an attitude of playfulness and because, in the case of the *World of Warcraft* participants, it occurs online, an assumption is often made that erotic role-play can be done with minimal risks to the self. As the second section of this chapter pointed out, however, the switching of frames during play can give rise to psychological and emotional issues that need to be managed. By showing how humour and mutual surveillance were strategically employed to help minimise risks to the self, this section provided evidence that erotic role-play contains inherent risks. In participants' assessment and management of these risks, however, it was found that not all risks are exclusively associated with the diegetic or player frames. There was a minimised presence of management strategies in erotic role-play situations where players had already been intimate in other frames. This suggests that rather than impede the inclusion of erotic themes in role-playing, intimacy with partners outside the game actually assisted in including erotic content inside the game.

The final section of this chapter addressed the types of relationships that develop from erotic role-playing. Because of ERP's sexualised nature, it might be assumed romantic, or at least sexual, out-of-character relationships would develop out of the game because of interactions within it. This, however, was found not to be the case. Every participant discussed erotic role-play as resulting in the building of friendships. Furthermore, the computer-mediated communication and physical distance between *World of Warcraft* erotic role-play partners seemed not to influence the development or sustainability of their friendships. During observation, both the *World of Warcraft* participants and the tabletop group gave and received gifts, celebrated out-of-character events such as birthdays and holidays, and communicated with one another outside the game through the use of mobile phones and textual messages. The main observable difference between the two groups, aside from geographical distance between ERP partners, was that the tabletop group met each other in-the-flesh before beginning to role-play. In finding such similarities between the two groups, not only is the reliance on binary distinctions between online and offline friendships questioned but also an argument is made for the consideration of erotic role-players as similar to any other hobbyist group. Just as players on a sports team might initially meet through a common interest in their chosen sport and then begin communicating outside practice times and matches, so too do erotic role-players.

NOTES

1. Vent is an abbreviation for Ventrillo, which is an auxiliary voice-chat program commonly used by MMO players to verbally communicate with one another.
2. This is not to suggest the themes participants erotic role-played with were then performed as part of their sexual behaviour – as the previous section has shown this is not the case – but rather it formed a type of foreplay that led to in-the-flesh sex.

7 The Future of Erotic Role-Play

Through ethnographic research, which used participant experiences as data and an abductive research strategy to interpret the data within researcher experience and theoretical texts, a detailed account of erotic role-play was provided in this book. In applying sociological theory to help explain the practice, erotic role-play was viewed within a larger social framework wherein its affordances to experiment with alternate economies of pleasure were considered. In doing so, the boundaries between online and offline, virtual and real, and mind and body were found not to be as clear or as separate as might have been assumed.

This book contributes to a growing body of research within the fields of games studies and game design that further deepens our understanding of how and why people play games, and how and why people interact through games. Of perennial interest, due largely to news headlines and moral debates about the function games should have within society, the controversial topic of sexual content in games is a useful one for highlighting the ways in which a particular culture views not only games but also sexuality. Whether or not sexuality can be considered playful or a topic made available for play is both controversial and debatable. As evidenced through the research presented here, however, an argument can be made that at least some adult role-players want to engage with sexual themes in their games. To review what these themes are and reinstate their importance to the research, the major findings of the research need to be reviewed below.

MAJOR FINDINGS

In order to gain a nuanced understanding of the phenomenon of erotic role-play, the research presented here assessed whether or not participants used it to experience sexuality outside normative routines. Additionally, in treating erotic role-play as different from cybersex or virtual sex, the research questioned the influence games' rules had on the inclusion or exclusion of content for erotic role-play. Finally, to determine if erotic play in virtual worlds effects real life outside it, questions were asked about how the activity crosses over into participants' real lives. This section will review each of the three research questions and their answers to summarise the major findings of the research.

The primary finding is that erotic role-play is used to explore non-normative sexuality. In their responses, participants discussed using erotic role-play to experience sexual acts and themes they found impractical, impossible, or undesirable in their everyday, out-of-game lives. The clearest example of this came from Caleb's writing of erotic stories that featured rape as a central theme for Megan. In Chapter Six, Megan and Caleb discussed how although rape scenarios were a sexual fantasy of Megan's, Caleb found it difficult to simulate the fantasy in-the-flesh. As a compromise, Caleb wrote stories featuring their role-play characters in situations of sexual violence as gifts for Megan. Through frame analysis, Caleb's comfort in writing about a topic he found uncomfortable in-the-flesh is read as being indicative of the separation of frames that occurs during play. That which is uncomfortable in the primary social frame becomes manageable in the diegetic, in-character frame.

Bolstering this assertion is a previous quote from Megan found in Chapter Four in which she discussed sexuality as a vulnerable and exposing experience for most people. When read alongside a quote from Random, which said that, for him, erotic role-play is an opportunity to have silly fun with friends, the idea emerged that the nature of play opens up sexuality to be explored through erotic role-play. The diegetic framework combined with play's silliness and frivolity allow the difficult, uncomfortable, or embarrassing aspects of discussing or exploring sexuality to become manageable. In erotic role-playing through a character, participants were afforded both a level of distance from their primary social frame, through temporarily inhabiting a character and performing actions through that character, and recourse to claim any unfavourable or non-normative actions were done playfully or in jest. So not only do erotic role-players use the activity to experiment with and express sexual acts outside of their routine but they do so through entering a space of manageable risk provided by the diegetic frame and play.

An additional aim of the research was to assess what effect, if any, the ludic elements of game worlds had on erotic role-playing. This question was asked not only to differentiate the act from cybersex and virtual sex but also to investigate whether or not the rule-structured nature of game worlds affected the themes and types of sexuality played with. Rules were found to paradoxically include and exclude sexual content for play.

For the tabletop group, knowledge of officially published player guides was central in dictating the themes available for play. The game texts themselves provided rules for the functional inclusion of sexuality by way of character abilities, such as seduction checks and Savage Genitalia, detailed in Chapter Five. Importantly, however, it was in the participants' interpretation of these rules that decisions to include or exclude content for play were determined. In the example in which Dan disciplined a player for attempting to involve sexual violence in a scene that he felt it was unwarranted, the importance of rules is further illustrated. Diegetic believability, or rather the framing of character actions within the context and social rules of a particular game world, was necessary for erotic content to be included. As Dan states in Chapter Five, just as he wouldn't expect a group of characters to 'stop and breakdance', he wouldn't expect sexuality to emerge out of nowhere. The other tabletop players supported Dan's comments and noted that for sexual content to be present in a game, there must be a reason and purpose relating directly to the game's setting and objectives. It is in this way that rules were seen as both encouraging and limiting erotic role-play.

Unlike player handbooks, which provided guidance on when to include and exclude sexual themes, the rules of *World of Warcraft* sought to ban erotic role-play from the game altogether. Most likely arising out of negative media attention and punishment from law or the Entertainment Software Review Board, the ban on erotic role-play in the game did not prevent the activity from occurring but rather spurred participants to find creative ways around the ban and create their own rules. Through the tactical use of built-in game functions such as group chats and whispers, participants were able to creatively find ways around the ban and continue to erotic role-play without facing disciplinary measures. However, lacking the tabletop group's rules for the inclusion of sexual content, the *World of Warcraft* participants needed to create their own to ensure they and their partners kept erotic role-play within the comfort of the diegetic frame. The guild's forums were central in the creation and maintenance of rules for erotic role-playing. Important concerns such as privacy, anonymity, exposure, and diegetic believability were all covered by the guild's rules, which were maintained and enforced by the guild leaders, officers, and members themselves.

Not all participants exclusively erotic role-played with other guild members, however, which meant they needed to create and enforce their own rules with potential partners. In two excerpts from Greenhat and Penpy, they implemented their own rules to ensure they and their partners kept erotic role-play manageable, safe, and within the diegetic frame. For Greenhat, this was done through conducting trial sessions with partners to ensure they were not 'one-handed typers' or merely seeking ERP to provide carnal pleasure. For Penpy, rules were put in place to ensure flirtations and emotions that emerged from erotic role-play stayed within the game and diegetic frame so as not to threaten the monogamous relationship he shared with his wife.

The exploration of the rules overall assists in understanding how erotic role-play functions within play and games. While play opens up sexuality to be explored in a way that limits the risks to the self, rules limit this exploration and the impact it can have. Unlike virtual sex or cybersex, wherein a type of sexual play is undertaken for sexual gratification, the rules of erotic role-play were enforced or created to ensure the activity stayed coherent within the narrative of the game world and the experienced affects remained within the diegetic frame of experience. As the findings in Chapter Five suggest, however, attempts to limit erotic role-play to the diegetic frame were not straightforward.

The final, major finding of the research is that participants found multiple pleasures in erotic role-play that troubled the idea of crossover. Although, as previously asserted, the rules of erotic role-play mandate character actions be kept within the diegetic frame, the constant management work of participants attests this was not always clearly or easily done. Participants' oscillation between character, player, and primary social frames demanded management of potential emotional and psychological issues that could arise. Although these issues were handled in part by rules, they were additionally managed through humour and mutual surveillance. Evidence for this came from a comparison between Scott's first erotic role-play experience with a group of players he was not intimate with at the time and Dan's experience where he was. As detailed in Chapter Six, humour was implemented to minimise the serious emotional implications of playing with uncomfortable or embarrassing aspects of sexuality within groups that had not previously broached sexual topics. In Dan's experience, where he was sexually intimate with a group of players, humour was absent. Having shared sexual experiences with other players in other frames, there was less need for Dan and the other players to minimise the potentially troubling emotions that might have arisen out of erotic role-playing.

Likewise, similar responses were found within the *World of Warcraft* group. For participants like Greenhat and Penpy, who were not intimate with their erotic role-play partners outside the game, rules needed to be developed and implemented to prevent threats to monogamy or discomfort within the primary social frame. This was not the case for couples Megan and Caleb, and Lamb and Grin. When real-life couples erotic role-played together, the act often became a type of foreplay or a precursor to in-the-flesh sex. Like the tabletop group, dealing with perceived risks in other frames meant sexual intimacy could be experienced in erotic role-play, which actually assisted in the inclusion of sexual content.

OVERTURNED STEREOTYPES

In addition to the major findings, the research also provided a detailed account of erotic role-play through the experiences of participants. This detailed account not only provides information about a population of players little is known about but also helps to overturn some stereotypes and assumptions made about the players and their reasons for erotic role-playing. As evidenced by the excerpt from the tabletop group in Chapter Six and the responses to ERP hotspots like Goldshire detailed in Chapter Five, within role-playing communities it is often assumed erotic role-players' primary motivation is carnal pleasure, and this pleasure comes at the expense of good role-play. Additionally, as the review of literature in Chapter Three pointed out, research on role-players has found them to be a psychologically burdened group that tend to be over-representative of racial, religious, and sexual minorities (Williams, Kennedy, and Moore 2010). Combing past academic findings on role-players as a whole with popular perceptions of erotic role-players results in a rather unfavourable portrayal of the group as marginalised thrill-seekers. In my exploration of the phenomenon, however, many of the assumptions associated with erotic role-players were overturned.

The idea that erotic role-players seek out the activity for carnal pleasure was contested in Chapter Five's exploration of the types of pleasure gained from erotic role-play. Through participant responses, the types of pleasure experienced by erotic role-players were found to fit three modalities: the contemplative reader, the experimenter, and one that almost fits the carnal-pleasure stereotype. The contemplative reader modality, exemplified by excerpts from Mocha and Cog, was by far the most common response to the question of why participants erotic role-play. Within this modality is the idea the pleasure of erotic role-play comes from the expression of creativity. The second most common modality was the experimenter who draws on insights. Both couples who participated in the research described the function of erotic role-play as not only a chance to express themselves creatively but also as a chance to experiment with things impossible or impractical in-the-flesh. As already mentioned, erotic role-play for these couples often filled the role of foreplay, eventually leading to in-the-flesh sex. Rather than be used as a masturbation aid, as the tabletop role-playing group assumed, for these couples erotic role-play was a chance to experiment with impractical or undesirable concepts and a way to 'get turned on' for their partners. The final modality is exemplified in Dirty's retelling of his favourite erotic role-play session. In the retelling, presented in full in Chapter Six, Dirty's favourite ERP experience resulted in the use of voice-chat software to express the sounds of masturbation. Although, in this singular example, masturbation is mentioned as factoring into Dirty's enjoyment of the experience, and this response exemplifies the stereotype of the erotic role-player, other parts of the interview helped to give perspective to this modality. When asked if he had ever done something similar in real life, Dirty questioned my use of the term 'real'. For him, erotic role-play does occur in real life. I interpreted Dirty's response as pointing out the unreliability of binary separations of terms such as 'real' and 'virtual'. For Dirty, both the event and its effects transcended the boundaries between virtual reality and reality. This example helps to illustrate the mind and body are involved in both real, in-the-flesh sex and in virtual, imaginary, erotic role-play.

In blurring the boundaries between embodied and imagined dimensions of sexual experience and their entwinement in diverse practices, Dirty's excerpt also helps in thinking about the ways in which such binary distinctions influence stereotypes. As previously mentioned, another stereotype of erotic role-players is they are bad role-players who allow their out-of-character desire for carnality to 'cross over' or 'bleed' into in-character interactions. Through detailing the multiple modalities of pleasure participants gained through erotic role-play, the research helped to disprove this stereotype. Additional evidence to refute the binary assumptions of in-character and out-of-character bleed stems from the absence of romantic relationships between players. If crossover were an issue and if erotic role-players were using the activity to fulfil an out-of-character desire, then we might assume out-of-character romantic relationships would develop between participants. However, this was not found to be the case. Every participant, including Penpy, who had to manage his out-of-character interactions, discussed erotic role-play ultimately resulting in the building of friendships. This was true of both the tabletop and the *World of Warcraft* participants. The similarity in findings between the two groups, despite differences in medium, suggests a pre-existing, unnecessary distinction between building friendships online and offline. Regardless of how the participants erotic role-played, they viewed the activity as building and strengthening friendships, which eventually led to out-of-character, out-of-game communication. The friendships between erotic role-players can be compared to those that develop out of any other hobbyist group.

The resulting profile of erotic role-players fits neither the popular stereotype of the carnal thrill seeker nor the academic findings that role-players in MMORPGs are a psychologically burdened group. As the research has shown, players gain multiple, alternate pleasures from erotic role-play and do not possess unrealistic expectations of what might result out of the activity. Just as friendships might develop out of any other hobby, so too do they develop out of erotic role-play. Furthermore, participants were able to manage the psychological and emotional burdens of oscillating frames and playing with uncomfortable and embarrassing topics, which would presumably be difficult for a psychologically burdened group. Although the population of participants in this study is too small to make generalisations or directly refute past academic research such as the Williams, Kennedy, and Moore (2010) survey of role-players, it is worth reporting none of the participants mentioned any negative emotional or psychological effects from erotic role-playing. As part of the standard interview and focus-group guide, participants were asked if they had ever encountered an erotic situation in-game in which they felt uncomfortable and whether or not they felt they had the power to end the situation. Although some participants, including the tabletop group, did mention feeling discomfort with certain topics, all reported they were able to handle the situation, either by logging off, talking to the offending player, or removing them from their play group. However, to truly get a full picture of who erotic role-players are and how sexuality, on a general scale, is interpreted by players of digital games further research needs to be conducted.

THE FUTURE

The available body of literature on sexual practice and games is growing, but currently insufficient to gain a nuanced and deep understanding of the relationship between games and sexuality. Beyond descriptions of sexualised female avatars (Taylor 2006; Pearce and Artemesia 2009; MacCallum-Stewart and Parsler 2008; Corneliussen 2008), vague mentions of in-character weddings and births (Taylor 2006; MacCallum-Stewart and Parsler 2008) or general laments over the digital-game industry's immature treatment of sexuality (Krywinska 2012; Gallagher 2012), there is a dearth of information about the ways in which games are used to explore sexuality and the effects this has on players. This book has made a contribution towards filling this gap in knowledge by focusing on erotic role-play as an example of an intersection between games, play, and sexuality. In providing a detailed account of how players use and manipulate games and rules, and the meanings they attribute to erotic role-play, a base of knowledge about the affordances of playing with sexuality in game worlds is established.

Although technology has changed since Turkle's (1995) study of virtual sex in MUDs, the act of typing in-character actions and reactions to erotic stimulus has not. As online games continue to develop in both graphic and narrative sophistication, there is reason to believe erotic role-play will develop with it. Since this research was conducted, the content of digital games has changed. In the span of only two years, games have changed what they are willing to include, even at the expense of more prohibitive review-board ratings. This inclusion of sexual content, which will be discussed in further depth below, has interesting implications for erotic role-players. As has been demonstrated here, players want and will find ways to include sexual content in the games they play, and will interpret and reinterpret existing sexual content as they see fit. Within the highly competitive market of the digital-games industry, it is unsurprising some of the more recent titles to be released actively include and incorporate sexuality. Although it might stand to reason the inclusion and acceptance of erotic themes and content within role-playing games should be an inherently good development for erotic role-players, other nuanced factors such as player agency and choice over representation are also important factors in audience reception.

ArenaNet's recently released MMORPG *Guild Wars 2* (2012), for example, includes references to sexuality and sexual preferences as parts of quest text, lore, and character backgrounds. Rather than assume all characters to be either asexual or heterosexual, *Guild Wars 2* features several prominent characters with same-sex partners. Likewise, ArenaNet has not shied away from including mild sexual content in questlines through the form of erotic novels the player must read to progress with the game. Additionally, the unique implementation of group-instanced role-play areas has answered the common complaint among erotic role-players that there are not enough private and romantic locations to engage in their favourite pastime.

Even more recent, *Elder Scrolls Online* (ZeniMax 2014) received a 'mature' rating from the Entertainment Software Review Board for, among other factors, sexual content in the game. As a major, highly anticipated release from a beloved series of single-player RPGs, the rating was unexpected. Blizzard actively tries to police sexual content like erotic role-play from player interactions to maintain their 'Teen' rating. Presumably this policing is done to prevent upset for players and parents and to maintain a larger population of gamers to pay monthly subscription fees. Rather than follow Blizzard's model and protest the rating, *Elder Scrolls Online* developer Bethesda accepted the decision (Makuch 2014). The game, which along with sexual innuendo features non-player characters engaged in bondage and domination play in the basement of the Ebony Flask tavern, explicitly engages with sexual themes in a way previous games have not. Taken as an example, there are certainly reasons to speculate that future role-playing games will look at *Elder Scrolls Online* as a game that did not shy away from the mature rating. Should the game be successful, in whichever way success might be defined, it could embolden future games to also not shy away from including sexually explicit content for fear of a loss of profitability.

With the change in the presentation of sexuality, from its minimised and censored presence in *World of Warcraft* to the more inclusive *Guild Wars 2* and *The Elder Scrolls Online*, there is reason to suspect player interactions and experiences will also change. With open inclusions of sexuality also comes defining examples of what sex is in the particular game world. Implicitly encoded as endogenous rules, what may appear as a liberating inclusion of sexual themes might actually be another form of regulation. Inherent within these changes are strategies of power and new tactical responses to attempts to control and regulate erotic role-play and these need to be investigated to deepen our understanding of games and sexuality.

Ludography

ArenaNet (2012). *Guild Wars 2*. Computer game, PC. Washington, U.S., NCsoft.

Blizzard Entertainment (2004/2010/2012). *World of Warcraft: Cataclysm*. (PC) Blizzard Activision: Irving, California: U.S.

Bridges, B. (1995). *Freak Legion: A Player's Guide to Fomori*. Black Dog Game Factory: Stone Mountain, California.

Campbell, B., Inabinet, S., McKinney, D., Moore, J., Achilli, J., and Skemp, E. (1998). *Book of the Wyrm*. White Wolf Game Studio: Stone Mountain, California, U.S.

Cook, M., Tweet, J., and Williams, S. (2002). *Dungeons and Dragons: Book of Vile Darkness*. Wizards of the Coast: Renton, Washington.

Gygax, G. (1978). *Advanced Dungeons and Dragons: Players Handbook*. TSR Games: Lake Geneva, WI.

Gygax, G. (1979). *Advanced Dungeons and Dragons: Dungeon Masters Guide*. TSR Games: Lake Geneva, WI.

Johnson, L. (2006). *World of Warcraft the Roleplaying Game: Horde Player's Guide*. Arthaus: China.

Marmell, A., Shomshak, D., and Suleiman, C. (2004). *Vampire: The Requiem*. White Wolf Game Studio: Stone Mountain, California.

Rein-Hagen, M. (1992). *Vampire: The Masquerade, first edition*. White Wolf Game Studio: location unspecified.

Rein-Hagen, M., Hatch, R., and Bridges, B. (1994). *Werewolf: The Apocalypse, second edition*. White Wolf Game Studio: Stone Mountain, California.

Volition (2011). *Saints Row: The Third*. Computer game: PC. Illinois, U.S., THQ.

ZeniMax (2014). *The Elder Scrolls Online*. Computer game: PC. Maryland, U.S., Bethesda Softworks.

Bibliography

Aarseth, E. (1997). *Cybertext: Perspectives on Ergotic Literature*. John Hopkins University Press: London.

Barton, M. (2008). *Dungeons and Desktops: The History of Computer Role Playing Games*. AK Peters, Ltd.: Wellesley, MA.

Belk, R. and Coon, G. (1993). 'Gift Giving as Agapic Love: An alternative to the exchange paradigm based on dating experiences'. *Journal of Consumer Research*. 20(3). pp. 393–417.

Bergson, H. (1956). *Laughter: An Essay on the Meaning of the Comic*. Translated by Brereton, C. Arc Manor: London.

Betcher, W. (1987). *Intimate Play: Creating Romance in Everyday Life*. Penguin Books: New York.

Björk, S. and Holopainen, J. (2003). 'Describing Games: An interaction-centric structural framework'. In Copier, M. and Raessens, J. (eds.). *Level Up – CD-ROM Proceedings of Digital Games Research Conference 2003*. Available from http://www.digra.org/dl/db/05150.10348. Accessed 05 June 2012.

Blaikie, N. (2000). *Designing Social Research: The Logic of Anticipation*. Polity: Cambridge.

Blatterer, H. (2013). 'Friendship's Freedom and Gendered Limits'. *European Journal of Social Theory*. pp. 1–22.

Boellstorff, T. (2008). *Coming of Age in Second Life: An Anthropologist Explores the Virtually Human*. Princeton University Press: Oxford.

Bowman, S. (2011). 'Social Conflict and Bleed in Role-Playing Games'. *Proceedings From Knudepunkt Annual Live Action Role-Playing Conference 2011*. Helsinge, Denmark.

Burn, A. and Carr, D. (2006). 'Defining Game Genres'. In Carr, D., Buckingham, D., Burn, A., and Schott, G. (eds.). *Computer Games: Text, Narrative and Play*. Polity Press: Cambridge.

Butler, J. (1990). *Gender Trouble*. Routledge: London.

Butler, J. (1993). *Bodies That Matter: On the Discursive Limits of "Sex"*. Routledge: New York.

Caillois, R. (1961). *Man, Play, and Games*. Translated by Barash, M. University of Illinois Press: Chicago.

Caldecott, S. (2008). 'Tolkien's Project'. In Caldecott, S. and Honeggar, T. (eds.). *Tolkien's The Lord of the Rings: Sources of Inspiration*. Walking Tree Publishers: U.K. pp. 211–232.

Campbell, J.E. (2004). *Getting It On Online: Cyberspace, Gay Male Sexuality, and Embodied Identity*. Harrington Park Press: London.

Caplana, S., Williams, D., and Yee, N. (2009). 'Problematic Internet Use and Psycho-social Well-being Among MMO Players'. *Computers in Human Behavior.* 25(6). pp. 1312–1319.

Charmaz, K. (2004). 'Premises, Principles, and Practices in Qualitative Research: Revisiting the foundations'. *Qualitative Health Research.* 14. pp. 976–993.

Consalvo, M. (2003). 'Hot Dates and Fairy Tale Romances: Studying Sexuality in Video Games' in Wolf and Perron (eds.) (2003). *The VideoGame Theory Reader.* Routledge: New York.

Corneliussen, H. (2008). '*World of Warcraft* as a Playground for Feminism'. In Corneliussen, H. and Walker Rettberg, J. (eds.). *Digital Culture, Play, and Identity: A World of Warcraft Reader.* MIT Press: Massachusetts. pp. 63–86.

Costikyan, G. (2002). 'I Have No Words & I Must Design'. In Mäyrä, F. (ed.). *Conference Proceedings of Computer Games and Digital Cultures.* Tampere University Press: Tampere, Finland. pp. 9–33.

Diamond, T. (2006). '"Where did you get that fur coat, Fern?" Participant observation in institutional ethnography'. In Smith, D. (ed.). *Institutional Ethnography as Practice.* Rowman and Littlefield: Oxford. pp. 45–64.

Döring, N. (2004). 'Feminist Views of Cybersex: Victimization, liberation, and empowerment'. *CyberPsychology & Behavior.* 3(5). pp. 863–884.

Dovey, J. and Kennedy, H. (2006). *Game Cultures: Computer Games as New Media.* Open University Press: New York.

Entertainment Software Rating Board. (2012). '*World of Warcraft Cataclysm Rated Teen*'. [Online]. Available from: http://www.esrb.org/ratings/search.jsp [Accessed 15 March 2012].

Finch, J. (1996). '"It's Great to Have Someone to Talk to": Ethics and politics of interviewing women'. In Hammersley, M. (ed.). *Social Research: Philosophy, Politics, and Practice.* Sage: London. pp. 166–180.

Fine, G. A. (1983). *Shared Fantasy: Role-Playing Games as Social Worlds.* University of Chicago Press: London.

Foucault, M. (1978). *An Introduction: The History of Sexuality Volume One.* Translated by Hurley, R. Vintage Books: New York.

Foucault, M. (1984). *The Care of the Self: The History of Sexuality Volume Three.* Translated by Hurley, R. Penguin Books: New York.

Fron, J., Fullerton, T., Morie, J. F., and Pearce, C. (2007). 'Playing Dress-Up: Costumes, roleplay and imagination'. Philosophy of Computer Games Conference, January, University of Modena and Reggio Emilia, Italy. Accessed 17 November 2014. Available from http://www.ludica.org.uk/LudicaDress-Up.pdf.

Gallagher, R. (2012). 'No Sex Please, We are Finite State Machines: On the melancholy sexlessness of the video game'. *Games and Culture,* 7(6). pp. 399–418.

Glaser, B. and Strauss, A. (1964). 'Awareness, Contexts, and Social Interaction'. *American Sociological Review.* 29(5). pp. 669–679.

Goffman, E. (1959). *The Presentation of Self in Everyday Life.* Penguin Books: London.

Goffman, E. (1974). *Frame Analysis: An Essay on the Organisation of Experience.* North Eastern University Press: Boston.

Gotterbarn, D. (2010). '"Perfection" is not "Good Enough": Beyond software development'. *ACM Inroads,* 1(4). pp. 8–9.

Gouldner, A. (1960). 'The Norm of Reciprocity: A preliminary statement'. *American Sociological Review.* (25) 2. pp. 161–178.

Griffiths, M.D. (2003). 'Video Games: Advice for teachers and parents'. *Education and Health*, 21. pp. 48–49.

Harviainen, J. T. (2012). 'Sadomasochist Role-Playing as LiveAction Role-Playing: A trait descriptive analysis'. *International Journal of Role-Playing*. 1(2). pp. 59–70.

Hine, C. (2000). *Virtual Ethnography*. Sage: London.

Holmes, J.E. (1981). *Fantasy Role Playing Games*. Hippocrene Books: New York.

Holmes, M. (2011). 'Emotional Reflexivity in Contemporary Friendships: Understanding it using Elias and Facebook etiquette'. Sociological Research Online. 16(1). p. 11.

Huizinga, J. (1949). *Homo Ludens*. Routledge: New York.

Jenkins, H. (2006). *Fans, Bloggers, and Gamers: Exploring Participatory Culture*. New York University Press: London.

Jet magazine (1953). 'New Game Called "7 Minutes in Heaven"', *Jet* magazine, 4 (13). 6 August 1953, p. 22.

Juul, J. (2005). *Half-Real: Video Games Between Real Rules and Fictional Worlds*. MIT Press: Cambridge, MA.

Kinney, D. (1993). 'From Nerds to Normals: The recovery of identity among adolescents from middle school to high school'. *Sociology of Education*. 66. pp. 21–40.

Kirkpatrick, G. (2009). 'Play Between Worlds: Exploring on-line game culture by TL Taylor'. In: Devine, F. and Heath, S. (eds.). *Doing Social Science*. Palgrave: Hampshire, England.

Klastrup, L. (2008). 'The Worldness of EverQuest: Exploring a 21st century fiction'. *Game Studies: The International Journal of Computer Game Research*. 9(1). [Online]. Accessed on 17 November 2014. Available from http://gamestudies. org/0901/articles/klastrup.

Kowert, R., Griffiths, M. D., and Oldmeadow, J. (2013). 'Geek or Chic? Emerging stereotypes of online gamers'. *Bulletin of Science, Technology and Society*. 32(6). pp. 471–479.

Krzywinska, T. 2012. 'The Strange Case of the Misappearance of Sex in Videogames' in Fromme and Unger (eds.). *Computer Games and New Media Cultures*, Springer Press.

Kuchera, B. (2014). 'The Cold War on the Adults Only Rating Must Stop if Gaming is to Grow Up'. 10 February 2014. Polygon. Accessed from http://www.polygon. com/2014/2/10/5397680/the-cold-war-on-the-ao-rating-must-stop-if-gaming-is-to-grow-up Accessed 29 September 2014.

Lenius, S. (2001). 'Bisexual People in a Pansexual Community.' *Journal of Bisexuality*. 1(4). pp. 69–78.

Lortz, S. L. (1979). 'Role-Playing'. *Different Worlds*. 1. pp. 36–41.

MacCallum-Stewart, E. and Parsler, J. (2008). 'Role-play vs. Game play: The difficulties of playing a role in *World of Warcraft*'. In Corneliussen, H. and Walker Rettberg, J. (eds.). *Digital Culture, Play, and Identity: A World of Warcraft Reader*. MIT Press: Massachusetts. pp. 225–248.

Makuch, E. (2014). 'Elder Scrolls Online rated M for sexual innuendo, severed heads, and drinking games', GameSpot, 27 February 2014. Accessed from http://www. gamespot.com/articles/elder-scrolls-online-rated-m-for-sexual-innuendo-severed-heads-and-drinking-games/1100-6417994/. Accessed 25 September 2014.

Mason, J. (2002). *Qualitative Researching*, second edition. Sage: London.

Mauss, M. (1990). *The Gift: Form and Reason for Exchange in Archaic Societie.* Translated by Halls, W.D. Routledge: London.

McCurley, M. (2010). 'Blizzard to Patrol Moon Guard's Goldshire for Harassment, Erotic Role Playing'. *Joystiq.* Available from http://wow.joystiq.com/2010/08/04/blizzard-to-patrol-moon-guards-goldshire-for-harassment-erotic. Accessed 28 April 2012.

Montola, M. (2008). 'The Invisible Rules of Role-Playing: The social framework of role-playing process'. *The International Journal of Role-playing.* 1(2). pp. 22–36.

Montola, M. (2010). 'The Positive Negative Effect in Extreme Role-Playing'. In: Mäyrä, F. (ed.). *Proceedings of DiGRA Nordic 2010: Experiencing Games: Games, Play, and Players.* University of Tampere Press: Tampere, Finland.

Morgan, D. L. (1988). *Focus Groups as Qualitative Research Methods Volume 16.* Sage: London.

Mortensen, T. (2008). 'Humans Playing *World of Warcraft*: Or deviant strategies?'. In Corneliussen, H. and Walker Rettberg, J. (eds.). *Digital Culture, Play, and Identity: A* World of Warcraft *Reader.* MIT Press: Cambridge, MA. pp. 203–224.

Murray, J. (1997). *Hamlet on the Holodeck: The Future of Narrative in Cyberspace.* MIT Press: Cambridge, MA. pp. 98–99.

O'Connell Davidson, J. and Layder, D. (1994). *Methods, Sex and Madness.* Routledge: London.

O'Leary, T. (2002). *Foucault and the Art of Ethics.* Continuum: New York.

Paccagnella, L. (1997). 'Getting the Seats of Your Pants Dirty: Strategies for ethnographic research on virtual communities'. *Journal of Computer Mediated Communication.* 3(1). Available from http://jcmc.indiana.edu/vol3/issue1/paccagnella.html. Accessed 7 May 2010.

Pearce, C. and Artemesia. (2009). *Communities of Play: Emergent Cultures in Multiplayer Games and Virtual Worlds.* MIT Press: Cambridge, MA.

Plummer, K. (1995). *Telling Sexual Stories: Power, Change and Social Worlds.* Routledge: London.

Poster, M. (1995). *The Second Media Age.* Polity: Cambridge.

Prozesky, M. (2006). 'The Text Tale of Frodo Nine-fingered: Residual oral patterning in *The Lord of the Rings*'. *Tolkien Studies.* 3. pp. 21–43.

Sicart, M. (2009). *The Ethics of Computer Games.* MIT Press: Cambridge, MA.

Smol, A. (2004). '"Oh…Oh Frodo!": Readings of male intimacy in *The Lord of the Rings*'. *MFS: Modern Fiction Studies,* 50(4). pp. 949–979.

Stark, L. (2011). 'Intro to Ars Amandi' in 'Leaving Mundania: Inside the World of Larp Blog'. Accessed from http://leavingmundania.com/2011/11/09/intro-to-ars-amandi/. Accessed 2 September 2014.

Suits, B. (2005). *The Grasshopper: Games, Life, and Utopia.* Broadview Press: Peterborough, Canada.

Sundén, J. (2012). 'Desires at Play: On closeness and epistemological uncertainty'. *Games and Culture.* 7(2). pp 164–184.

Sutton-Smith, B. (2001). *The Ambiguity of Play.* Harvard University Press: Cambridge, MA.

Taylor, T. L. (2006). *Play Between Worlds: Exploring Online Game Culture.* MIT Press: Cambridge, MA.

Turkle, S. (1994). 'Constructions and reconstructions of self in virtual reality: Playing in the MUDs'. *Mind, Culture, and Activity.* 1(3). pp. 158–167.

Turkle, S. (1995). *Life on the Screen: Identity in the Age of the Internet.* Simon and Schuster Paperbacks: New York.

Wachowski, E. (2007). 'Blizzard Disbands Extreme Erotic Roleplaying Guild'. *Joystiq*. Available from http://wow.joystiq.com/2007/09/17/blizzard-disbands-extreme-erotic-roleplaying-guild/. Accessed 20 May 2011.

Westbrook, L. (2010). 'Erotic Role-Play Police to Patrol World of Warcraft'. 5 August 2010. *The Escapist* magazine. Accessed from http://www.escapistmagazine.com/news/view/102598-Erotic-Role-Play-Police-to-Patrol-World-of-Warcraft. Accessed 2 September 2014.

Williams, D. (2006). 'A (Brief) Social History of Video Games'. In *Playing Computer Games: Motives, Responses, and Consequences*. Eds. Vorderer, P. and Bryant, J. Mahwah , NJ : Lawrence Erlbaum Associates, Publishers. pp. 197–212.

Williams, D., Kennedy, T., and Moore, R.J. (2010). 'Behind the Avatar: The patterns, practices, and functions of role playing in MMOs'. Games and Culture. 6(2). pp. 171–200.

Yee, N. (2006). 'The Demographics, Motivations, and Derived Experiences of Users of Massively Multi-User Online Graphical Environments'. *Presence: Teleoperators and Virtual Environments*. 15(3). pp. 309–329.

Index

146 *Index*

For Product Safety Concerns and Information please contact our
EU representative GPSR@taylorandfrancis.com Taylor & Francis
Verlag GmbH, Kaufingerstraße 24, 80331 München, Germany